The Courage To See

Daily Affirmations For Healing The Shame Within

Deborah Melaney Hazelton

Edited by
Michael E. Miller

Health Communications, Inc.
Deerfield Beach, Florida

Deborah M. Hazelton, M.A., Ed.S.
InnerSight Unlimited
265 S. Federal Highway
Suite 125
Deerfield Beach, Florida 33441

Publisher: Health Communications, Inc.
          3201 S.W. 15th Street
          Deerfield Beach, Florida 33442

Cover design by Vicki Sarasohn

Dedication

This book is dedicated to Lyndi, my working guide dog, who came to me from the South-Eastern Guide Dogs training school in Palmetto, Florida. She continues to enhance my courage to see by safely guiding me through life's open spaces, and teaches me what true commitment and relationships really mean by her constant loving spirit and demanding child-like ways. She is my teacher and my child.

Acknowledgments

A book that is so personal would not be complete without saying thanks to those individuals who have supported me. Some have helped directly, others indirectly, a few may not even know how their lives, personally and professionally, have influenced my work, my attitudes, my spirit and my creative process. To each of you who have believed in me, I humbly offer my appreciation.

To the members of my family for offering support in their own individual styles, and for pushing the buttons that motivated me over the years to keep on seeing and expressing myself: Mom, Em, Judy, Rick, Jenny, Wendy and all the cats who have come to mean so much as I grow in my own ability to experience the joy of loving and living today.

To the staff at U.S. Journal and Health Communications, one of the most interesting and amazingly hard-working group of people I've ever known. Gary Seidler and Peter Vegso, especially, have tremendously motivated this book. From them I have learned more about business, team work, success, learning to work with and through fun and conflict. Gary Seidler, most particularly, has been a close friend and an important mirror and messenger for me spiritually.

To Jeffrey Laign and Andrew Meacham, the editors for *Changes* magazine, who have been my buddies for many laughs, discussions, debates and other forms of sanity-restoration when needed. Jeff has also been a patient and loving teacher of writing.

To several U.S. Journal Training faculty members who have offered personal and professional support to me in this process. They include: Robert J. Ackerman, Joseph R. Cruse, Jane Middelton-Moz, Robert Subby, Sharon Wegscheider-Cruse, Joy Miller, Mary Lee Zawadski, Rokelle Lerner, John Bradshaw, Ruth Fishel, Sally Baker and many others.

To those additional authors, trainers and speakers who, by their work, have served as mentors — thanks to: Sid Simon, Patricia Sun, Louise Hay, John Bradshaw, Tom Sullivan and Meg Christian. Your pioneering and creative works have helped me to find my own courage to see and be myself, in personal and professional endeavors. And the teachings of the Unity Church, especially the writings of Eric Butterworth, the meditation style of Rosemary Rhea, and the friendship, work and everyday examples of Charles and Betty Lelly.

To Marilyn Volker, one of the most helpful and affirming friends I have ever known; and Suzanne Anderson, a loving and powerful gift to have crossed my professional and personal paths. These women are two of the most exciting, vibrant and supportive women to have influenced my personal and professional definition and style. Their courage, clarity of insight and willingness to speak out have added special dimensions of validation to who I am and what I do.

To Dr. Ann Gustin, who was the therapist who helped me to see and make great strides in my own growth process by being able to reach and see beyond my defenses.

To Lois Adler for her concept of "Getting A New Fan Club."

To Jill Boyd, the first person to teach me about alcoholism and recovery, who has been a long-time friend and is part of numerous examples and stories in this book.

To the staff at SouthEastern Guide Dogs, especially Mike Sargeant, who helped me to take my teammate Lyndi in hand and move more courageously and fully into the wide-open spaces to claim my life. Mike's influences particularly helped me to believe and live with more integrity as a woman who happens to be blind.

To Sharon and Dave Chapnick, and the folks at Florida Software for keeping my computer in working condition. Most especially Sharon who, with her friendliness, spirit and skill, supported me through the process of this book by enthusiastically reading it and putting parts of this manuscript in working order.

To Michael E. Miller, my editor and partner on this book (and with InnerSight Unlimited), as well as friend, teacher and co-worker with the U.S. Journal. I am thankful for his belief in me, for trusting my courage to see and for the learning we have both gained daily about what being partners really means.

To the friends and acquaintances who have been part of my journey and whose spirits have been with me in completing this manuscript. In some cases, their technical mastery has kept me reaching to learn more. Their friendships, humor, insight and existence as role models continue to serve as landmarks that give me support and a sense of personal connectedness. They include: Chris Gray, Vinnie Rappa, Rick Alfaro, Kevin Kitchens, Marsha Arthur, Doug Hall, Nancy Burgess-Hall, JoAnn Hendelman, Gayle Krause, Paul Edwards, Ron and Valerie Manning, Betty Potter, Tommie Dayton, Steve Dresser, Dr. Michael Marshall, Deborah Morris and Lee Jones.

To all those guardian angels who have been in just the right place at the right time to make the difference, even without knowing who you were.

To those of you who will read this book and continue to find your own courage to see.

And finally, to myself for following my own inner sight, listening to the voice within and living with courage.

Contents

Introduction

Imagine working in the field of co-dependency, adult children's recovery and personal growth for several years and feeling like you were supposed to wait for somebody to give you permission to write a book. This is just one of the memories behind completing this first book of mine, *The Courage To See*.

I teach what I learn and learn best by teaching. And I tend to believe that this process is much the same for most of us pioneering humans. The continuing lessons we need to experience are the same ones we will no doubt find ourselves teaching. Hopefully we will expand our learning even further through the process we teach. We all need to find the courage, the inner light and fortitude to see and know whatever is true for ourselves. Be it an opinion, an intuitive hunch, a dream, a fear . . . it takes courage to see and to stay awake as the world continues on its merry way.

Personal and professional aspects of my life have significantly contributed to the factors that have set the tone for what you will read in this book. The most important among these are that I have lived with blindness since birth, I am an adult child, I am a licensed mental-health professional, I am a woman, I am a spiritual being. My life represents each of these dimensions separately and I am more than all of these combined.

What This Book Is About

"Seeing" is about getting through shame, knowing you are separate from any low self-esteem you have been carrying. Shame is that limiting piece that says "I'm not okay, I'm not worthy." This book is not about *finding* courage. You have lived with and survived your pain for years. Your courage has already been tested, you need only to recognize and honor that which is already yours. *The Courage To See* is about healing the shame within, moving forward with inner sight and wisdom to reap the fullness of yourself and your life.

How To Use This Book

Within many of the 12-Step programs there is a saying which goes, "Take what you like and leave the rest." That is my intent with *The Cour-*

age To See — use what makes sense for you. This book is "about me," and it is "for you." It is up to you to decide when and if it is "for you." Not only will you likely disagree with me in places, but even I disagree with me sometimes. There are contradictions, and so life goes.

The Format

There are 366 entries, one for each day of the year. Each entry has three components: The Affirmation, The Reflection and The Meditation.

The Affirmation is a summation statement that you can take with you, write down, hear in your own head if you want to. Affirmations are like training wheels. They are merely one of many tools for bringing about a place of knowing.

The Reflection component has insights and personal experiences that come from my life experience. I offer them to stimulate your thoughts, to suggest possibilities and simply to share one more perspective.

The Meditation section is a place where you can go deeper into your own experience, taking whatever piece, or peace, from this quiet time that is best for you.

A Final Note For The Journey

I wish you continued courage as you stretch to see and know who you are and what your life is about. I wish you healing that sets you free from the bondage of shame.

God bless you.
— D.M.H.

> *The Affirmation — Through growing beliefs and actions, I move out of convenient ruts towards fulfillment.*

The Reflection — How many times have you found yourself remaining for a long time in a convenient rut: a job, a relationship, a geographical location, a pattern? You know better but it's hard to take the necessary steps to do anything about it. At the same time, you feel the restlessness that comes from knowing that place is not really you. But when you've lived with shame, chaos and fear of failure, a sense that you don't deserve what's best for you, convenient ruts offer the illusion of security.

The Meditation — Today I begin to recognize the illusive trap of security for the sham it is. As I have the courage to see the convenient ruts in which I have been stuck, I feel my wings spread as I take risks to move out of them and on to greater freedom and meaning.

The Affirmation — I dare to know, believe and express the quantity and quality I desire and deserve in my relationships and in my life.

The Reflection — "It's quality that counts . . . quality time, quality intimacy, quality life," we say, when we want to make sure we're not caught wanting too much. So we strive to make the most of each mouth-watering morsel, to be grateful. It's wonderful to feel grateful, to make the most of each opportunity. But why assume an either/or position — quality or quantity? Why not assume it's okay to have both?

The Meditation — I want quality in my life and I want lots of it. I take time to be honest with myself first about how much I really want. My old feeling of shame tells me I may be a burden or unlovable. This is a new time and I deserve to be true to myself about what I need, desire and deserve.

The Affirmation — I take care of myself on a regular basis.

The Reflection — Taking care of yourself isn't (or at least shouldn't be) a haphazard affair you can only do when you feel like it. That little child within doesn't go away when you have an adult-sized body or you think you're behaving in totally adult ways. The little child can be a best friend who monitors and signals your need for anything from a nourishing meal to emotional support.

The Meditation — Today I listen and am willing to take the time to understand what my child within has to offer for my needs for self-care. To stand securely as an adult requires deliberate effort to take care of myself. The lack of self-care in my past has been yet one more way I did not treat myself with deserved worth and respect. The self-care I offer myself today is an important act of self-love.

The Affirmation — Today I will emotionally reveal a part of myself that is important to me.

The Reflection — What does intimacy mean to you? For many of us, the magic of romanticism has been intriguing if not deceiving. "Finally," so has gone the hopeful scenario, "someone will fill the void and answer my needs." Beyond the intoxication of that sort of fantasy lies the real nuts and bolts of intimacy-making. Emotionally revealing ourselves is the main ingredient. It means vulnerability, letting someone in and daring to let ourselves come out of hiding.

The Meditation — Today I do not need to be in a hurry about relationships. I have an entire lifetime to discover how to achieve greater intimacy. Yet each day is another opportunity to take at least one more small step towards learning how to become more intimate, how to slowly reveal small parts of myself.

The Affirmation — I will use my anger as an energy source to fuel the course of action I know I must take.

The Reflection — How do you feel about yourself when you know you're angry? Is there a familiar discomfort about expressing your anger today? Most of us don't learn how to allow our anger to work for us. It can be a wonderful monitor to let us know when something is wrong and change is in order. It can also be used to empower us once we've decided it's time to act.

The Meditation — Today I remind myself that I am fully entitled to all my feelings, including anger. I set aside the negative messages from my childhood and recognize anger now as a cue that I can use to prompt necessary change in my life. Its acceptance as part of my emotional process is as valid as any other feeling. Beyond acceptance, my choices are to decide how best to express my anger, to whom and for what reasons.

The Affirmation — I can do better at asking for the help I need from others.

The Reflection — Asking others for emotional help in our lives can be difficult. The gamut of emotional help can run from basics like needing a hug or a willing ear, to seeking professional help. In any case, it means taking a risk, daring to say, "Yes, this is who I am right now." Then it's a matter of trusting that the other person will respond to you with as much integrity as you had honesty about your needs.

The Meditation — Today I remind myself that admitting I need some help, especially emotional, is an important reflection of how far I've come. I know there will be risks in honestly expressing those needs. But each time I take these risks, I reduce my sense of isolation by strengthening my connections to people who will respond to me with integrity.

The Affirmation — I think wisely before I make promises or commitments to myself or to others.

The Reflection — In alcoholic or other addictive households, promises are frequently made to cover remorse and further perpetuate denial. If we grew up in such households, our frame of reference for knowing how to make commitments is not grounded in reality. We may only be used to knowing that "if I tell someone or even myself that I will do something, I can get off the hook." We still have our own remorse or conscience to live with.

The Meditation — Today I think responsibly about the promises I want to make. I can set reasonable goals to accomplish. Asking myself what is behind my impulse to make a promise can help me understand the tendency to make promises and commitments that won't come through, while working toward keeping the ones which will.

The Affirmation — All I have to do is be "slightly willing" and the universe will joyfully help me do the rest.

The Reflection — Sometimes when a new change is hard to make, it's easy to believe you have to be totally willing to make the change before you take action. But that sort of either/or thinking can be used as a highly convenient excuse for doing nothing. Being slightly willing is like opening the door or the window and letting just a little bit of light in. It is better than complete darkness.

The Meditation — My Spirit within is more than adequate to help make the changes that are for my greatest good. I have found that if I open the door ever so slightly, all the other details, including my wayward attitude, are somehow brought together so that harmonious change is natural and comfortable.

The Affirmation — I am at one with my-self when I honestly say what I mean.

The Reflection — If you're too busy saying what you think others want to hear or what will gain you the approval or acceptance you're seeking, you're simply not telling the truth. How about those meals you ate more than once because someone thought you liked that particular food? What about the gifts you felt guilty about not liking? After a while, those kinds of half truths catch up with us and leave us feeling fragmented, discon-nected and isolated.

The Meditation — Today I listen to what I'm saying to myself and others. Do I really mean something other than what comes out of my mouth? Am I saying what I think I *need* to say in order to survive the situation? This pattern developed out of survival and has continued out of fear. Now I can use my growing aware-ness and self-forgiveness to gradually turn my behavior around.

The Affirmation — I find reflections of myself in the mirrors represented by the people with whom I interact.

The Reflection — Our involvement with other people presents us with numerous lessons for our growth. Others can tell us a lot about ourselves when we pay attention to the intensity of our reaction to them. It can show us just how unfinished we are with behaviors or reactions from a past relationship.

The Meditation — Today I can look in the many mirrors afforded me and decide what I want in my life and what I am ready to discard. For instance, I can work more on getting beyond my own negativity, try on new behaviors, communicate differently and take new risks instead of reacting out of old, painful, familiar patterns. In short, I can do my spiritual homework by learning many lessons from the mirrors of others on a daily basis.

> *The Affirmation — I use the fullness of
> the vision that I know is truly possible
> from within my mind's eye.*

The Reflection — When we talk with each
other, whether in person or over the phone, we
frequently say "Oh yes, I see." No one really
gives it a second thought until we ask a blind
person, "Do you *see* this?" All of a sudden, the
people asking the questions forget that they
use the term many times, but not for physical
seeing. "I *see* your point," "I *see* it (I understand it) this way."

The Meditation — Vision is in the mind. It em-
bodies our ideas, perceptions, beliefs through
which we act or react. We can choose to recognize and broaden our vision or we can assume
it consists of only the physical and the concrete. Ideas have come from vision. Inventors,
creators of all sorts began with vision, seeing
the possibility.

*The Affirmation — I trust the divine tim-
ing of the universe to help me work out
the details of my life.*

The Reflection — It has taken most of us a lot
longer than a day to realize that things don't
usually happen overnight. The best of change
is often gradual. When it does come bubbling
in a great rush, it doesn't generally carry the
kind of positive meaning or growth enhance-
ment that lasts. When I feel impatient about
making a change right now, I ask myself what
the sense of urgency is all about. "What do I
need from this change that I don't have within
myself right now?"

The Meditation — Some of the best changes
happen to me when I quit looking over my
shoulder or holding my breath. It's as though
my Higher Power decides to give me what I
want when I least expect it. I can relax in the
flow of life, knowing that slow change is healthier and less stressful.

The Affirmation — I've survived every crisis in my life, often in spite of myself. I can learn to give the same credit to other survivors.

The Reflection — Watching others deal with challenging circumstances is one thing — living through my own is quite another. I can let my imagination drift and project myself into the plight of someone else. This affords me a certain luxury I don't have time for when faced with my own challenges. It is one thing to assume how much of a struggle someone is going through and quite another to review how we have survived our own.

The Meditation — Today I honor the fact that I have survived every one of my own crises. These moments have served as platforms from which I have taken new leaps of growth, awareness, faith and courage while building my inner strength. I cannot walk in someone else's shoes, but I offer them the respect of survivorship.

The Affirmation — I can use more of what I have waiting to be discovered right here in my own backyard.

The Reflection — It is easy to see the abilities of others and assume that they are naturally better because of some circumstance or luck in their life. When I think that way, I impose unfair limits on myself, forcing distance between me and the person I'm placing on a pedestal. Not only will I eventually get a sore neck, but I will also fail to notice the resources, talents, skills and abilities that lie right below my own feet.

The Meditation — Today I recognize that I have used as many of the tools and abilities I needed to survive and live my life in the best way I have known. And my experience has shown me that I am a survivor. The backyards of my life are filled with many treasures waiting to be discovered and used to move beyond survival.

The Affirmation — I expect to be well used.

The Reflection — It is one thing to be used; it is painful and self-deprecating to be misused. Many of us know what it is to experience burnout, frustration and rage from feeling misused by others. Motivated perhaps by the hope of earning the love, approval and acceptance we crave, we have inadvertently set ourselves up for being misused.

The Meditation — Though I don't want to be misused, I know there are still healthy and abundant ways for me to be used or to be useful. I don't have to try too hard. As I am open to being used in positive ways, I learn to fine tune my ways of discerning what is useful and what is not. I learn to distinguish what is my need for someone else's good and what is their own. As I let go of old ways to change and control others, I am at less risk for setting myself up for being misused.

> *The Affirmation — Now I am reaping
> without ruining.*

The Reflection — Many of us have felt riddled
with shame and low self-worth for so long that
we don't know how to stop blaming ourselves
and rubbing our noses in the real or imagined
mistakes we have made. If we learned to fear
punishment or abuse as a child, it may be hard
to believe we have the right simply to enjoy the
good things coming into our lives today. It's
time we let ourselves off the hook.

The Meditation — I can take hold of the present moment and firmly yet gently remind myself
that I am not locked into nor doomed to live in
the past. I can learn to trust my abilities to live
and act in healthy ways. While everything I
touch may not turn to gold, everything is not
ruined either. I can choose to not let the shame
and low self-worth I have lived with determine
the course of my future. The harvest of self-
esteem is mine to reap.

The Affirmation — I have more recipes and important ingredients for relationships available in my life today than ever before.

The Reflection — Our relationships are like recipes. The ingredients called for today might not be the same as yesterday's or last year's. As I grow and change, as I continue to discover who I am, I find I can throw some ingredients away. At the same time, I am learning to reach for new items to add to my recipe. I can take risks testing my taste buds, learning the range of possibilities I have for defining and meeting my needs.

The Meditation — My needs, my recipes for relationships in the past, were based upon ingredients that are toxic to me now. Today I will look at my recipe and make a new shopping list, based upon what I need now and the ingredients required for healthy relationships.

The Affirmation — Today I will identify one significant aspect of my life that is truly mine.

The Reflection — Those of us who have struggled with feeling abandoned know the pain of living on eggshells. Not unlike a book we've checked out of the library, we fear that at any moment the person, the activity, the cherished object will have to be taken back. Abandonment leaves us with the feeling that nothing is ever really ours to keep. So it is in relationships.

The Meditation — Today I will declare my experience as something that is truly mine. I have learned that while I cannot control people, places and things, the recollections, the feeling-memories and the images of the experience will never have to be returned, cannot belong to anyone else. In honoring those experiences I am better able to eliminate the fears of abandonment in my life.

The Affirmation — I allow myself to be teachable. I am open to making mistakes and learning from them.

The Reflection — What does humility mean to you? I used to think it meant giving up self-esteem. Most of us developed strong defenses. Anytime anyone would try to challenge our plans or beliefs, we often only held on more tightly. Not only does this sort of arrogance keep us from learning what we need to from our mistakes, it can cut us off from the very people who could teach us.

The Meditation — As a terrified child in a catastrophic and/or dysfunctional home it was unsafe to not know the answers. It was not okay to act and feel like a beginner. In turn, I got to be extremely good at faking, pretending to know, winging it to cover a sense of uncertainty. I became masterful at thinking on my feet. Today I do not need to hold on so hard, I learn more by letting go.

> *The Affirmation — I welcome and use self-pity as a signal. It tells me I am ready to make and receive changes in my life.*

The Reflection — We tend to think that self-pity is a negative thing. It's no fun to get stuck in the rut of depression; nobody enjoys someone who's always whining and complaining. When we were little children, the message of "Don't feel sorry for yourself" tended to go hand in hand with "Don't feel; don't be yourself." These messages only helped to feed our sense of shame.

The Meditation — My little child is clever at knowing what I need, when I am hungry for my life to move even more on track. If there wasn't any self-love inside me, there would be no reason for my child to believe I deserve my circumstances to improve. Rather than scold my child, I can listen to the signal of self-pity in order to bring about deserved change.

> *The Affirmation — I am willing to work on the delicate balance of responding to my own and others' needs.*

The Reflection — Many of us who grew up in homes where selfish behavior was either completely indulged or harshly prohibited. As adults, this can leave us without a comfortable midpoint or sense of balance. Having lost ourselves in other people, activities, possessions, chemicals, food, is it surprising that we resent the needs of others with so much anger? Or that we should hold our own needs in such disdain and disfavor?

The Meditation — Today I seek to develop a sense of responsibility with respect to my needs and how I respond to other people. There is no single formula for achieving balance. It takes time and practice, facing the vulnerability of my own needs, finding appropriate boundaries and responsible handling of my anger.

*The Affirmation — I take responsibility
and credit for the choices I make.*

The Reflection — We are always making
choices, through deliberate design or inad-
vertent circumstances. Likewise, we are always
dealing with the consequences or effects of
our choices. The people I spend time with,
the thoughts I think — all these have an effect
on my present and future circumstances. We
don't have the luxury of not making choices.
Our only choices involve taking responsibility
and credit for our decisions.

The Meditation — Today as I consider choices
that are mine to make, I quietly reflect on the
consequences of those I made yesterday. I am
learning, becoming more finely tuned in my
awareness of the choices I make and their
effects on my life and the lives of others. As I
embrace more fully my right and responsibility to make choices, I am freer to prosper
from the positive outcomes of learning.

The Affirmation — I let the results of some aspects of my life serve as feedback for other aspects.

The Reflection — There is an inter-relatedness throughout my life. I can see ways in which my physical health is affected by my emotions as well as the food I eat. In turn, I can look at my patterns of eating food and spending time, and ask myself if these have a resemblance to how I feel about myself or live out my relationships. For example, do I eat fast? And do I in turn, try to gobble down as much of a relationship as possible so I won't be hungry later?

The Meditation — I know now that I can use the feedback from certain aspects of my life as grist for the mill of personal growth. I cannot ignore those reflections which may be relevant to other aspects of my life. Yet I must also be careful to not make more of something than it is.

The Affirmation — I accept and appreciate the ideas that come to and through me.

The Reflection — Sometimes, all it takes to get a new change going in your life is a simple idea. You may not even know exactly from where or whom it might come. Everything that has been accomplished began with an idea. Some ideas seem to come in split seconds, yet they bring about major life changes. Others develop over time, perhaps in small steps that bring us closer to the final version that can really make a difference.

The Meditation — I can take time to appreciate the ideas which have already taken positive effect in my life. Even in the midst of a confusing, chaotic childhood, I have never been without the resource of my own invention, creativity and inspiration. Whatever they may be, I remember to appreciate my own ability to receive and use ideas.

The Affirmation — I am learning to make clear choices about what is true and right for me.

The Reflection — As a child, it often felt like it was necessary to be what "they" wanted me to be, no matter what. As time went by, I learned that certain other people might also like me "if only I would . . ." Most of us know only too well what little difference our efforts to meet such vague and ill-defined expectations made. When we take care of ourselves, those efforts don't necessarily have a profound impact on other people, either.

The Meditation — I don't have to take the world the way in which it is handed to me. While I may have grown up believing this was expected of me, I'm my own parent today and can make my own rules. As a child I had little choice but to live by the rules, decisions and options of Mom and Dad. Today I live more comfortably in the kingdom of my own choices.

The Affirmation — In moments when I feel pain, I trust it as an invitation to find out more about who I am and what I need.

The Reflection — As children we often got the message that our feelings did not count. So what possible good could they be — then or now — if no one would support us? Many of us learned to look for comfort and relief outside of ourselves. And all too often in our lives today, we are capable of deflecting and distracting ourselves from the sources of our pain.

The Meditation — Today it is important that I honor the self-love that is part of what has brought me this far. As I go through the essential pain, I am recovering treasures that got buried along with all those things I had come to believe were unacceptable. I let my pain guide me into renewed celebration of my life.

The Affirmation — I think carefully about the secrets of others I agree to keep.

The Reflection — If you grew up in a household where honest communication was a rare commodity or where you felt repeatedly left out, you may have learned to believe that being trusted with someone's secret was a sign that you were special or okay. But carrying the secrets of others may not be as glamorous as it once seemed; it means a commitment to silence. It means remaining isolated from common conversation with others in order to uphold the promised loyalty.

The Meditation — I remind myself to clearly discern whether the responsibility to keep others' secrets is in my best interest to accept. Will this entail a silence that keeps me isolated from others important to me? I weigh carefully how much time and energy I give up to this secret that could be better spent taking care of myself.

The Affirmation — I affirm my sexuality beyond gender, roles and expectations.

The Reflection — Experiencing our sexual energy doesn't mean that we in any way must act out sexual impulses with or through our genitals. Sexual energy is directly connected to our spiritual essence. This is partly why we feel such profound shame when our sexual boundaries have been violated and our spirits are left with massive wounds in them.

The Meditation — The energy I experience as I am open spiritually can in no way be expressed unless I open up to what I feel within and beyond my body. I seek today to set aside some of the shame I have felt about my body, the fears I have felt about opening myself up to the full experience of all my energies. I am not the vulnerable child I used to be and can integrate a stronger sense of safe boundaries in my openness to life.

*The Affirmation — I get involved with
spirit in my life.*

The Reflection — What does spirit mean without the assumptions of organized religion? We
find phrases like "team spirit," "holiday spirit"
or hear the moods of others described as "He's
in good spirits" or "Her spirits are low." In
short, the word often connotes a certain mood
of life or one's degree of liveliness.

The Meditation — As I move through this day,
I can call upon my spirit, my sense of life
inside me, to heighten my levels of "response-
ability." My spirit within has been a continuous
source of strength for my survival. My spirit,
my spiritual nature, my spiritual being, my
spiritual needs, my spiritual growth . . . all
emerge as I move closer to understanding my
true self and celebrate the divinity of the child
who lives within.

The Affirmation — I take responsibility for having an appreciative fan club.

The Reflection — Do you find it hard to believe that it's okay to have a fan club? Some of us have been so used to feeling that we simply have to accept whatever crumbs and leftovers of support come along that we dare not rock the boat by saying what we really want or need. If we've lived with this victim syndrome, we may not feel entitled to surround ourselves with supportive people, either as friends or intimate partners.

The Meditation — Today I give myself full permission to have a fan club. I deserve to have it filled with people who love and appreciate who I am, what I need and where I am going with my life. To do anything less is an act of self-abuse I no longer need in my life. I seek people I can count on and will offer my dependability in exchange for membership in my fan club.

The Affirmation — Today I will practice healthy protection.

The Reflection — The child within each of us today still needs healthy protection. If we were violated as children, then no one was around to teach us not to violate ourselves. The sad truth is that many of us were violated by those adults we had trusted to provide us a safe, protective environment. Essential to our recovery, especially in resolving our shame, is the creation of our own places where healthy protection is available.

The Meditation — Today I make a commitment to stay alert to my inner sense of when I am violating myself. Self-violation is a mirror to my still struggling self-esteem. As I take risks to gradually trust the spirit inside to protect me while I am daring to be myself, I can move beyond the old temptations to violate myself.

The Affirmation — I clear out the crumbs in my life and set a table that offers more complete self-nourishment.

The Reflection — As a child, I got used to settling for crumbs, especially when it came to getting my emotional needs met. I was so hungry that it was more important to take what I could get. My appetite of unmet needs and low self-worth combined in such a way that it wasn't possible for me to say, "Wait a minute, I am worth much more than crumbs."

The Meditation — I have allowed people to answer my needs by throwing a few crumbs at me. Somewhere in the past I learned to believe that this should be enough. Today I remind myself that nourishment is a major key to emotional satisfaction and healthy living. If I tolerate crumbs, they will continue to monopolize the menu of my life. As I remove the crumbs in my life, my table is set with full nourishment.

The Affirmation — *It is safer for me to make mistakes and be more successful in my life as an adult.*

The Reflection — Often the driving urgency to be perfect is being propelled by a little child feeling unsafe, maybe somewhat out of control. When small, our only leverage in the chaos at hand was to try to gain control by being as perfect as possible. "If I am perfect, maybe they will like me . . . won't abandon me . . . won't criticize or violate me."

The Meditation — Today I can remind myself that I am an adult, not bound by the whims and wishes of others. If I don't have the approval of someone, perhaps it is an opportunity to learn to give myself my own approval. Wanting perfection is wanting protection. When I feel the drive to be perfect, I can usually find just below that sense of urgency a rigid script that says I need perfection just to survive.

The Affirmation — I pay attention to my eating habits and let them tell me how I feel about myself and my relationships.

The Reflection — Early on, food has carried emotional meaning for so many of us adult children. Depending upon the relationships and the atmosphere around us, it may have served as emotional contact, comforting presence in the face of abandonment, nurturance and a form of acceptance. The availability of junk food may have come to mean the answer to our emotional hunger, especially if it was readily available when nourishing people were not.

The Meditation — Today I notice how I eat and how its patterns carry over into my life. Have I craved love to the point that I have got used to eating fast? Do I crave attention so much that I eat whatever crumbs and junk come along? I can see to it that I have healthy portions of nourishing people and food in my life as I move towards balance.

The Affirmation — I forgive for myself.

The Reflection — My unwillingness to forgive others or myself is a measure of my struggling self-worth. Holding on to resentments and blaming tells me that I'm afraid it will be my only ticket into deserving my fair share. Being told to forgive others merely feels like being told not to feel. Forgiveness is both a central and somewhat controversial aspect of recovery. And it is a stepping stone towards healing that cannot be pushed any faster than the river is already moving.

The Meditation — When I forgive for myself, I set myself free. I'm not continually bound to unhealthy memories and circumstances. I can totally alter my perception when I forgive, let go of whatever continues to be a source of resentments in my life. I will seek and offer forgiveness at my own pace, in my own time.

*The Affirmation — I am learning to ap-
preciate and respect the love behind the
authority from those who care about me.*

The Reflection — As a child, I didn't know the
difference between punishment and abuse.
Without a healthy base of trust, it was out of
the question that any authority I experienced
was meant to be loving. Abuse felt like punishment; punishment was just more abuse. I am
reminded of this when I'm tempted to react
with intense emotion to authority.

The Meditation — As an adult today, I take
pride in learning to nourish and manage my
life in ways that are whole and healthy. I'm not
afraid to reach out and listen to the authority of
others as they offer me what they know, see,
believe or feel. I can learn from others. I can
practice healthy authority as I decide what is
most right for me.

The Affirmation — I can choose what I will and will not take in to my self.

The Reflection — As a dependent child, I was not free to decide what I would and would not take in. I had to swallow food I didn't like, absorb words that chipped away at my self-esteem, stuff feelings. Just as the food I eat affects my daily health, so do the internalized messages from others. If I repeatedly swallow putdowns and verbal abuse from others, my emotional health and self-esteem will gradually erode and my immune system will weaken.

The Meditation — Today I notice when I have swallowed something — food or someone's verbal message — that doesn't agree with me. Getting rid of it is not half as beneficial in the long run as learning from my patterns. I may want to watch my habits with sugar if I know I have a weakness for sweetness in life.

The Affirmation — I choose to treat my-self with the same respect I treat other people and their property.

The Reflection — Some things belong to the library and to other people; we usually don't put too much of ourselves into library books, write in them or on them, bend them or treat them as our own. When I don't have to return something or someone, I'm not afraid to bend their ear once in a while or make my mark in or on them. I don't have to ask permission, sign them out or pay attention to the due date, afraid I must eventually return what never belonged to me.

The Meditation — For too long in my childhood I was told to treat other people and things with more respect than I gave myself. I now recognize the implied message that I wasn't deserving of the same respect. Today I remind myself that the person I must respect most is myself. Without that I have no foundation for trust, self-worth and integrity.

The Affirmation — My self-esteem is my reputation with myself and I will work to strengthen it every day.

The Reflection — There is a quote: "What other people think of me is none of my business." Perhaps this is a good vantage point from which to work on freeing ourselves from having our self-worth dictated by others. When it comes to self-esteem, that definition of self that carries with it the full implication of who you are at the very core of your being, the opinion that counts is yours.

The Meditation — As I scan the landscape of my life course since childhood, I have no choice but to recognize how hard I have struggled on my journey to shore up the foundations of my self-worth and build a good reputation with myself. Today regardless of the storms I have to weather, my self-esteem can support an honorable reputation with myself.

The Affirmation — Today I give myself permission to find the courage and celebrate being a beginner.

The Reflection — Do you remember as a child being told to do something only once and then, when you didn't get it right the first time, being scolded and chastised? Children are so curious, so eager to learn. Yet the courage and adventurous spirit of a child can be so easily squelched. For many of us today, it is hard to dismiss these childhood scenarios when it comes to being a beginner and trying something new.

The Meditation — Today as I grow closer to understanding and appreciating the child within, I consider the source of strength and courage my child spirit has been. Curious, inquisitive, eager to learn . . . I did not lose these dimensions of my child spirit though sabotaged in an environment that could not tolerate imperfection. Each day on my journey, it has been that courageous child taking the awkward steps in recovery.

The Affirmation — My life and times are valuable and precious gifts I cannot afford to waste.

The Reflection — Do I waste time, hoping my life will finally begin when certain "other" things finally start to happen? Maybe I also waste possessions, or more importantly, some of my own gifts and talents? But as we embark on the journey into and through recovery, there is an acute level of awareness of the fullness and the richness of life. It's an appreciation that life has no dress rehearsal.

The Meditation — I open myself today to the movement and energy inherent in the life forces of the universe. I am a valuable individual with precious gifts to offer. I need to first honor my own aliveness and my appreciation for the fundamental process of moving towards my highest good. With this openness, I know it is not possible to waste any of my precious gifts.

The Affirmation — I am free to decide when being "nice" is appropriate for me.

The Reflection — Many of us grew up being indoctrinated about how it was always important to be nice, no matter what we were really feeling. If my inner child learned to believe I would be okay as long as I didn't ruffle any feathers, then I probably learned a lot about how to hide my true self and little or nothing about how to handle conflict. "Be nice" as an automatic rule is, for all intents and purposes, synonymous with "don't be."

The Meditation — Today I am learning that I don't have to be nice all the time. I am able and willing to be honest about my experience rather than merely gloss over situations and keep peace with others at all costs. It no longer helps to hide my true self or to let conflicts rob me of my serenity.

The Affirmation — I'm removing myself as an active member of the "clean-up committee" and meeting my own needs for a change.

The Reflection — Survival for many of us is always being on the "clean-up committee," helping everyone else to have a party. We learned to take control, fix the broken lives of others. One crisis after another, we soon learned how to live and give without a turn at receiving. Getting off the clean-up committee takes courage. It means putting out the message: "Here I am!"

The Meditation — It's time for me to get off the clean-up committee. I have been wading through the mess of broken lives and guilt-ridden messages from others for too long. There is more than enough work to do on my own behalf. I do not need to fix other people or their lives to feel good about myself any longer. It's enough to take care of myself.

The Affirmation — In choosing who I want to be close to, I listen to the totality of what I want.

The Reflection — Once I heard a woman say she wanted someone to have sex with but she didn't want him to hug or be affectionate with her. I chuckled to myself, trying to imagine having sex from only the waist down — just the mechanics. If you don't want people to know what's in your heart or to touch you in affectionate ways, what makes you think you would want to be in bed with them?

The Meditation — I listen to my body's responses as a whole when I imagine being close to various people. I respect my desires and dislikes and ease up on any old tendency to push myself into what I think I should like. I have a right to approach my participation in loving relationships as a whole person and do not need to fragment myself.

The Affirmation — I am learning to love who I am and deserve to give myself a valentine.

The Reflection — For years when I was a little girl, my mother gave me my own small heart-shaped box of chocolates for Valentine's Day. I carried it around all day, slowly eating the chocolates and felt pretty damn special. Then one year she insisted I offer some to a house guest. I knew it — I was angry — the box wasn't really mine after all. Years later in therapy, I bought myself the largest box of candy on Valentine's Day I could find. That one I did share with friends. This time it was my choice, not someone else's urging.

The Meditation — Today I take time to recognize, honor, celebrate and strengthen the primary relationship in my life — with the true inner self I am growing to know and respect. I mark the specialness of my being in some unique way on Valentine's Day.

The Affirmation — I take a moment to sincerely ask for help in communicating in the most honest and loving way.

The Reflection — Many times we have ended up in those emotionally intense, awkward situations where we are convinced that we won't be able to find anything to say. Or we've been afraid of saying the worst thing possible and sabotaging a situation with our anger or mistrust. When we have expressed willingness within ourselves, it's amazing how the right things suddenly do get said. I walk away with a feeling of tremendous gratitude.

The Meditation — In those moments when it is difficult to know how to respond, I go to a higher place within me and sincerely ask for the help I need. I will always trust my essential nature to be moving towards my greatest good. I could not have predicted that I would have said as much as I did or in the loving way that it was expressed.

The Affirmation — When I let someone into my life, I feel bigger than life.

The Reflection — By continuing to hang on to what is predictable and staying safe, I never find those people and experiences that take me beyond myself. I only fail to enhance the capacity for growth and disrupt the natural celebration of life that can lead to joy. It is through fully loving relationships that we come closer to embracing the spiritual beings we are meant to be.

The Meditation — When I dare to come out of hiding and let myself be known, when I allow another person to make a difference in my life, it's as though a new addition was just built on to my house — I have so much more room for new decor, new activity. When I let someone add their own special touch, I am never the same again. I am led further away from that old and predictable place of childhood.

The Affirmation — *I claim my life and my responsibility for being the person in charge of taking care of myself.*

The Reflection — A friend of mine and I were in the grocery store one day when she asked, "You do like French dressing, don't you?" I thought, "Should I be honest here or polite?" I said, "I'll eat it if it's what you usually have but I really am not fond of it." Her response was, "Oh good, I don't like it either." We saved ourselves from wasting a bottle of French dressing that neither of us wanted, and we saved energy not trying to needlessly please the other.

The Meditation — Each day I learn more about how to care for myself. How many times have I been afraid of others' reactions to my decisions, only to find out later that they were not biased negatively at all. I recognize today that as I actively claim taking care of myself, I am less prone to base decisions on assumptions unwarranted in the first place.

The Affirmation — I am better at accepting that some things get better when they change.

The Reflection — Sometimes it's the simplest of gestures that can gently open the door to change. I remember the transition from kindergarten to first grade as a change that was made easier by a special teacher. Everything in the new classroom was different relative to the kindergarten room. As I wandered around the room, trying to get comfortable, this new teacher calmly reassured me, "This isn't kindergarten. Things are different now."

The Meditation — Today I consider the constant process of change as it continues within and around me. I cannot alter my internal rate of change any more than I can either speed up or slow the current of a stream. I have choices to make about getting comfortable, and can gently remind myself that some things get better when they change.

The Affirmation — My body belongs to me.

The Reflection — Getting violated, abused or exploited as a child creates a twisted framework of beliefs that your body is not your own, that it's more available to others than to yourself. This is also the perfect set up for never learning about your boundaries. It's a process that annihilates the spirit, self-worth and sense of identity. Is it any wonder that we end up having health problems and twisted relationships?

The Meditation — Today as an adult I responsibly notice when I am violated by anyone. I pay equal attention to ways I am tempted to violate myself. Even as a child, I recognized the inner voice of discomfort, uneasiness and disease about what was happening to me. Now I can listen to that special voice seeking to warn me about violation and use it as a signal that it's time to pay attention to some of my boundaries.

The Affirmation — I get into the habit of listening carefully to what I really want.

The Reflection — It seems reasonable to expect that I could get what I really want about half the time. But if I'm only half-way honest about what I really want and am only receiving half of what I actually ask for, then it translates into getting only about one-fourth of what I really want in and from life. Why are we so tempted to compromise or settle for what other people might want for us in their own "helpful" way?

The Meditation — Today I begin to build the ledger to account for what I truly want in and from life. How much am I willing to invest in myself instead of depositing anger, resentments and guilt-debits in the bank of my own self-worth? As I get more honest with myself, I no longer have to settle for one-fourth of my dreams.

The Affirmation — I give up the false pretense and isolationist thinking that what other people say to and about me doesn't matter.

The Reflection — We do not each live unto ourselves on islands. We are affected by what others say and don't say. The choice is in what to do with the feelings once we know we are experiencing them. Assuming that no one can hurt us is a convenient way to stay in denial. Demanding that everyone live on egg-shells around us is a way of staying stuck in blame instead of using our reactions as platforms for healthier choices.

The Meditation — Today it's important to recognize and consider my beliefs about self-protection in recovery. As I grow less vulnerable to other people's opinions, my self-worth emanates from within. Yet I know I am not an island, nor do I want to be that isolated. I am free now to choose how much weight I grant to others' opinions.

The Affirmation — I give those I care about my unconditional respect.

The Reflection — I may not always understand the motives of people I care about, but I can honor their decisions and their expression. Respect doesn't have anything to do with agreement or disagreement. It doesn't necessarily have anything to do with understanding. It is simply honoring the right and integrity of another individual even if you may not agree with the particular choice an individual makes.

The Meditation — I have consideration for the people I respect. Respect comes from strength. Respecting others allows me to get my own agenda out of the way and give them room to be who they are. I can respect another and still take care of my responsibility to fulfill my own goals and desires in the personal growth process.

> *The Affirmation — I will survive my pain
> and take courage from these experiences
> to live more fully.*

The Reflection — It's one thing to think about
feelings, name them or imagine what it's like to
experience them and quite another to actually
go through the process of feeling them. The
process reconnects me with an awareness of
just how human I really am. I can use this
experience to give myself more credit for the
gains I've made, for the crises I've survived.

The Meditation — Today I fully acknowledge
my survivorship as testimony to the pain
through which I have opened the doorway to
recovery. I use the experience to accept and
empathize with the pain of others. Pain is an
inevitable, natural part of living but doesn't
have to become the uniform to wear in recovery. A willingness to experience it when it
surfaces is one way I affirm that indeed my life
is truly my own.

The Affirmation — I celebrate my worth in the activities, relationships and possessions of my life.

The Reflection — I can remember spending years believing that securing what someone else had was a sure measure of my worth. My own list of acquisitions and accomplishments wasn't enough. The doubt still lingered. "Maybe the people who want you are the rejects in this world. Get someone's love who already loves someone else and you'll know you must be worth something." That's living on borrowed time, an unrewarding existence.

The Meditation — Today I relish the ways I spend my time with the people who are in my life not by accident, but by my choice and theirs. I credit myself with what I have come through and beyond. It is time to enhance my healing from the feelings of low self-worth and shame instead of seeking self-measurement through others.

The Affirmation — I accept those things that work for me.

The Reflection — Learning to be little adults as children, many of us did our best not to need anything. Accepting help meant giving in to the feeling that we were shameful. Taking care of my child within means I am willing to be honest about what I need and what works for me. Accepting support and help in my life gives me the opportunity to accept myself beyond today. I am free to bask in this present moment, allowing my life to work for me. My inner child is nourished by life in this way.

The Meditation — I look around at the resources I may not be using. I notice opportunities I've previously chosen to ignore. As I gradually open to consider each one, I see the possibility of renewal and expansion in my life.

> *The Affirmation — I have the right to decide what is true and best for me.*

The Reflection — As a child I got caught up in having to protect myself from others. I needed to guard against the possibility that they would abandon me and I needed to protect myself from the abuse. Today I may still feel tempted to respond to others from a horizon of fear. Feeling guilty if I don't respond to others' whims and wishes and talking in ways that minimize the risk of potential abuse are patterns left over from the past.

The Meditation — I need to consciously remind myself that my body, my time, my energy, my beliefs, emotions, ideas, preferences, needs and desires belong to me. Today I make it my agenda to be in charge of myself and experience who I am in the present moment.

The Affirmation — I spend my time responsibly.

The Reflection — Waiting for time to pass is allowing time to be wasted. Time wasted is life lost. In childhood it was important to survive. If survival meant time merely passing, finding ways to kill time, that may have worked then. Today there is a price to pay for time wasted. If you feel as though your life and time always seem to get away from you or that you can't wait for time to go by until . . ., then setting priorities and learning time management are good skills to consider.

The Meditation — My time is my own to spend. That means it has value and there is a price to pay for my choices. I decide those things that are important. How much time do they take? I focus my full attention on planning the wise use of time.

The Affirmation — *My child is safe. I know who I am today and I am at the center of my present experience.*

The Reflection — Once I was trying to describe for a friend an unpleasant experience I had. It was one of feeling taken advantage of by someone who thought it was funny and justified. I was describing my anger and suddenly asked, "Do you ever get that dizzy feeling?" We both laughed in recognition of that overwhelming, disorienting anxiety we feel when trapped in a vulnerable situation.

The Meditation — Today I recognize the dizziness from terrifying times of childhood where again and again the emotional rug was pulled from under me. When they happen now, I can do more to take care of myself. I can take time to breathe. It's okay to not know all the answers immediately. I can give myself time to become centered in the present moment of my life.

> *The Affirmation — I do not indiscriminately cut myself down, up or off. I acknowledge the life inside of me and I pull out the weeds that get in the way.*

The Reflection — Once when deciding to get into therapy, I described my experience this way: "There is all this interference in my head. It's like having to think clearly and speak loudly to be heard above the noise of a roaring lawn mower." I looked up the word mow in the dictionary; it said "To kill indiscriminately." I loved the definition, for that was how I felt. When the lawn mower would be on, anything and everything I wanted, thought or felt was being cut down or indiscriminately killed.

The Meditation — Today the lawn mower is a signal that I'm feeling driven by old shame-based messages. Learning to separate from the past, to become my own parent so that my child today can receive healthy messages is part of a recovery process.

The Affirmation — I am actively aware of and involved with the communication that goes on in my relationships.

The Reflection — Imagine you're listening to someone talking to you. You're in tune with what's being said and suddenly something doesn't feel right. It's as though it just went "clunk." It's an interruption in a flow of information. What do you do with the clunk? Clunks that are not dealt with become "kinks" between us that distort messages.

The Meditation — Today I create safe ways to communicate my experience. I choose those friends with whom I can dare to bring up those unmentionables of the past when they encroach on my life today. In places where there are too many unresolved clunks or kinks, I sometimes choose to sever the relationship. Catching clunks before they become kinks means I need to take some risks in communicating.

> *The Affirmation — I consciously choose to move beyond the temptation to judge and criticize others.*

The Reflection — It is so tempting to criticize and judge others. Just when you get something figured out it feels so nice to self-righteously sound off about how someone else is doing it all wrong. It may be a way of cementing and boosting your own self-confidence, but as a habit pattern it will bring you to a deserted road.

The Meditation — All those places where someone else's values don't register comfortably with your own can help you decide what your values are. So often adult children move from a life-style of pleasing others to one of judging self-righteously. I look more closely now to see another path between these two options that has to do with learning to define and express what is true for myself.

> *The Affirmation — I practice self-for-giveness as a regular part of taking my own inventory.*

The Reflection — Did you ever think that self-forgiveness was something you would only have to do one time and then it's done forever? I continue to be amazed at how often I need to practice self-forgiveness. It's not one of those things that you can think your way through. It takes emotional muscle from the inside.

The Meditation — Today I believe that as I am truly able to forgive myself, I have no need to hold on to resentments toward other people. This does not mean that I condone what others do or have done. It means holding on to anger and criticism of others can be a way of avoiding how I feel about myself at any given moment. Practicing self-forgiveness sometimes means swallowing some grandiosity about perfection.

> *The Affirmation — Competence is a
> strong asset of mine.*

The Reflection — As an adult child who survived
a lot of things you are adept at accomplishing
many things as an adult today. At the same time
you have a big appetite for other people's help
and a deep need to know you're loved. The old
myth has it that people who are strong and
competent aren't supposed to have too many
needs. How could they be so insecure as to
need to know they are loved by others?

The Meditation — I am a person who has
accomplished a lot and given a lot from my
own talents and abilities. I am also aware that
I need a lot of care. I continue my struggle to
break through the myth of being strong and
totally independent, knowing it takes less courage to live out the myth. Letting others know
my needs and vulnerability is the biggest leap
forward I take into recovery.

*The Affirmation — I am able to be loved.
I am wanted by and desirable to an
unlimited number of people.*

The Reflection — Was love of who you were as
a child sparse? Somewhere along the line you
had a difficult time with loving yourself. Consequently, you got used to thinking that you
don't deserve to or are not able to attract the
love you crave. Role models with a lot of love
in their relationships were not plentiful, if available at all. Now if you are looking for a partner,
you may not even believe that as an adult you
are lovable.

The Meditation — Look in whatever mirror you
choose and practice knowing that today you
are an adult, a woman or man, not bound to
past patterns or definitions. You are not bound
to anyone else's dictating as to how much you
are allowed to receive.

The Affirmation — I am power-filled.

The Reflection — What does it mean to be power-filled? Recovery programs say we need to accept our powerlessness. Does coming to know ourselves as power-filled have to conflict with this? I don't believe so. Accepting powerlessness is useful when we need to reach beyond ourselves and allow new answers to come. But using powerlessness, punishment or shame as ways to keep the boat from rocking becomes another manifestation of our "dis-ease."

The Meditation — Today I have the right and responsibility to claim my power-fullness. Power-filled, I have survived many challenges and crises and grown beyond thus far. I can creatively plan and implement the quality of life I desire and deserve today.

The Affirmation — I love you to wholeness.

The Reflection — Don't diminish someone by claiming to love them to pieces. Instead, love them to wholeness. Our language feeds our underlying beliefs and subsequent behaviors. If you see others in reducing ways, you will treat them accordingly and you will receive reducing results in return. Most of us feel broken down inside enough as it is, where life sometimes chips away at us piece by piece. We can take a first step by noticing our words, our beliefs and daring to put aside those small pieces and loving in a much bigger way.

The Meditation — As I change my language, uncovering any limiting beliefs, I may find that my behavior changes as well. Becoming more detached in ways that are healthy, giving people room to feel their feelings and make their choices lighten my own burden.

The Affirmation — I can always grow in loving myself more.

The Reflection — "The problem with her is she likes herself . . . She knows she's pretty . . . His ego is too big . . . He has such a big head . . . He thinks too much of himself." How do you feel when you read these statements? Most of us end up somewhere between being self-righteous and shame-filled. When we were little, statements like that were used to bring us under others' control. It is no wonder then that they hone in on that old insecurity.

The Meditation — Today I set aside my anger and self-righteousness, recognizing that these postures in others may stem from their feeling insignificant and isolated. Today I know that true self-love is not possible when it is coupled with my willingness to be vulnerable. I acknowledge my fears of boosting my own self-esteem.

> *The Affirmation — I bring the best of myself to my relationships.*

The Reflection — What does it mean to bring the best of yourself to relationships? For some people this may strike a negative chord that sounds like one more setup for burn-out. It used to mean always taking care of the other person, always giving whatever it took to make someone else happy. But bringing your best to a relationship means first establishing your best sense of self. Sacrificing your self to a relationship will ultimately undermine the best you can hope to truly give.

The Meditation — Today, bringing my best to relationships means staying in touch with my heart and retaining my integrity. When I am truly loving and honest, I remain connected as a whole person. The truth is always manageable when I speak from my heart.

> *The Affirmation — I actively assume the responsibility to not settle for crumbs consciousness.*

The Reflection — Do you ever feel you don't deserve quite as much as the next person? Or that you should not want so much in your life? Crumbs consciousness means you believe you are meant to settle for less. "Don't complain," "Don't make a mountain out of a mole hill," "There's always someone worse off than you," are typical statements built on a platform of low self-worth and doubt that fosters crumbs consciousness and defeatist thinking.

The Meditation — Today I watch the temptation to settle for crumbs — crummy food, crummy or crumbly relationships, crummy salary, crummy health or crumbly self-esteem. This thinking is not good enough for me any longer. I need to take the risks to get the nice big helping I deserve instead of the leftovers in my past.

The Affirmation — *I will not resort to talking or thinking in terms of trying. I decide to do or not do.*

The Reflection — Saying "I'll try" is a safe way out just in case of failure or fear. It is scary at first to say "I'll do," or "I won't do." "What if I don't come through?" goes the fantasized scenario in our heads. Whatever happened to flexibility and realistic goals?

The Meditation — Today, as I grow more able to say "I will do" or "I will not do," I know I am beginning to reclaim my sense of power. It means I am a "response-able" person. If circumstances change, if I change my mind, then so be it. That's better than wiggling in and out of situations in a sort of invisible way and staying safe, but also remaining plain and unrecognizable. I am more ready to give up the isolation that comes from trying.

> *The Affirmation* — *I begin lessening the influence guilt has in my life by using it as a window to see what other emotions are lurking in the background.*

The Reflection — On my coffee table, I have this novelty bottle of "Guilt Away" spray. It lists more things to feel guilty about than even I could have imagined. It's filled with rose water so that the user can go away smelling like a rose. Of course, I don't use the spray personally — I'm afraid I'd use it all up. Then I'd feel guilty about that. But the "guilt away" spray doesn't help me with the feelings that hide behind my guilt.

The Meditation — When I habitually feel guilty, I can begin to ask myself important questions — Who am I mad at? What am I disappointed about? What is making me angry and resentful? As I seek answers to these questions, I will withhold judgment and self-criticism. The windows must remain open if I am to find understanding of my own patterns.

> *The Affirmation — Shifting gears does not threaten my sanity, my well-being or my sense of direction.*

The Reflection — The confusing, chaotic experiences of your childhood can leave you with some strange and painful messages about plans shifting and not getting what you want. You may have learned to believe that when plans shift, you just aren't worthy, your life is out of control and there is no hope. It's time to derail yourself from this old track of thinking. You may be surprised to discover a sense of lightness, flexibility and competence that comes from shifting gears.

The Meditation — I recognize today that there have been times when plans have shifted faster than I am comfortable with. I remember to back off and consider my life in the larger picture. As I heighten the focus on my life today, I am able to pay less attention to messages from childhood. I create new opportunities as I learn to shift gears.

The Affirmation — I take responsibility for claiming my experience in the present and calling it for what it is.

The Reflection — The child within deserves to be recognized, heard and understood; that is a part of the recovery process. At the same time, the recovery journey is meant to lead you forward toward a fulfilling and healthy life. To couch your present experience in phrases like "My child needs . . .," "My child wants . . ." is a convenient way to hide behind it and avoid being a responsible adult. It takes more guts to say "I am feeling . . ., I am needing or wanting . . . ." It challenges your self-esteem because it requires you to move in the direction of integration.

The Meditation — It may feel safer to refer to the child in vulnerable moments, but I know it is only a first step in identification. The next step is integration. Now I give myself permission to move forward and claim all the parts of who I am in this present moment.

The Affirmation — *I strive for the essential balance between awareness and living that is important for moving further in my personal growth.*

The Reflection — Awareness and insight are important in bringing about desired changes in our lives. However, they are only the beginning steps. I liken them to learning how to balance a book on one's head. The real trick is figuring out how to walk forward and not lose the book. Without the specific practice of new ways to move forward, such awarenesses are nearly useless.

The Meditation — Today I prepare myself to move forward with the natural process of growth by building from the foundation of insights, awarenesses and experiences. My vision of a path to step onto is clear. But I know that change will only come as I move. And movement in any direction will be more productive now as I seek the balance between awareness and living.

The Affirmation — I turn off the analysis and get on with life.

The Reflection — It is one thing to come out of hiding, to unravel and open up old pain and old treasures. This journey we call recovery has done much to help us claim our pent-up energy and positive potential. It is quite another matter to become weighed down by recovery. People can get caught up in the process as though they have an imaginary medicine chest, constantly diagnosing what is wrong with themselves and everyone else.

The Meditation — Today I begin giving myself permission to stop being sick and start living my life. My child within doesn't need to be gripped with fear and weighed down with censoring and analysis. I can now embrace the truth about who I am inside, my inner self and can use this truth and its strength to start living my life.

The Affirmation — *It's okay to have expectations. My job is to be clear about my agendas when I have them.*

The Reflection — In our childhoods many of us learned to deny our expectations, usually in response to being told we were too demanding. It's not easy to erase that old tape about how you shouldn't be selfish or want too much. The trick is to expect a whole lot for yourself. At the same time, it's wise to know what you expect *from* yourself and others, as distinct from what you expect *for* yourself in the big picture.

The Meditation — Today I take time to consider carefully and appreciate where I am in my life, respecting my strengths and limitations as I understand them. But I also keep myself entirely open to the prospect of deeper understanding and change. I work to refine and clarify expectations in my life — of others, from others, for myself and from myself.

The Affirmation — I don't need to resort to blame in discarding relationships or relationship patterns that are not good for me. I am free to decide what I want and need.

The Reflection — It's so easy to place blame. The powerful people in our lives threw blame around to make sure they had the last word, were in control. We learned that to be seen as powerful and in control we could and should use blame. Using blame is like another temporary high that, for a few moments, points the finger and takes the focus off ourselves.

The Meditation — This is a new day, a new time. I no longer have to live with the old rules of my childhood house. There are relationships and patterns within them I no longer need. I set aside blame as a basis for deciding in my relationships and claim the power and responsibility for getting my needs met honestly without blame.

The Affirmation — I set the limits of my responsibility at the far edge of where they belong — with myself.

The Reflection — Sometimes, just getting clear on the fine line between concern, nurturance and appropriate caretaking versus over-responsibility is hard. Assuming too much responsibility for others may be a part of the tendency to blame. The thinking goes something like, "If I can just find enough wrong with them, maybe I won't have to remain so responsible." Ultimately, the one thing you will no doubt have to be responsible for is making the decision to end the relationship.

The Meditation — Today I take time to understand that my tendency to be over-responsible in relationships is an outgrowth of yet unresolved dimensions of my self-esteem. I am worth loving and can begin making choices based on my own needs, desires and experiences. This is the true responsibility I have to myself.

The Affirmation — I believe in seren-dipity.

The Reflection — You never know what opportunities are right around the corner from you even at this very moment. All it takes is a thought, a seemingly simple idea, a chance conversation, being in the right place at the right time. No matter how hard you rehearse, how much planning you do, there are always things that happen out of the ordinary at some of the least likely times, from some of the most unlikely people.

The Meditation — Regardless of whether I choose to perceive certain events in my life as mere coincidence, destiny or unavoidable, I can remain confident that today is not a carbon copy of yesterday and tomorrow can never be a duplicate of today. I do not know what might happen — that is the essence of serendipity in my life and the universe. I live with a simple willingness to put one foot in front of another and be delightfully surprised by the positive outcomes.

> *The Affirmation — I open up windows with my laughter.*

The Reflection — Laughter is like a rush of fresh air and a warm beam of sunlight all rolled into one. It gives us a sense of detachment when that's needed, a break from the intensity of hard work, a change of perspective. Laughter, when it comes from deep inside, is one of those rare uninhibited moments when we let our bodies get fully involved in our experience. Laughter also makes it hard to remain isolated from other people.

The Meditation — Today I expand my awareness, sensitivity and receptiveness in ways that reduce any tendency to self-watch, or be unfairly judgmental so that I can bring more laughter into my life. In laughter I find myself experiencing a greater sense of lightness, I'm more connected to other people and I enjoy a better sense of balance. Laughter helps me move beyond myself without losing a sense of self.

> *The Affirmation — I enjoy a healthy out-
> look on my time alone and do not use it
> to create or hide behind walls.*

The Reflection — For the majority of us, one of
the things recovery means is learning how to
balance our needs for spending time alone
with being around other people. We can learn
a lot about ourselves by spending time alone.
But too much solace in solitude can be a way
of remaining isolated as we hide behind walls.
The secret is to keep a balance and get clear
on what it is we're looking to get out of our
time alone.

The Meditation — Today I look to examine and
redefine if necessary my need for time alone.
Does my time alone add to a sense of isolation?
Or do I somehow feel more connected to parts
of myself that are easier to access when I am
not distracted? I trust my ability to communicate honestly when I need to and choose silence when that's what feels most comfortable.

> *The Affirmation — I let my spirit be transformed with the magic of humor.*

The Reflection — Have you ever noticed what a wonderful sense of release humor provides for us? Suddenly strangers don't feel so awkward, tensions are not so silent and secretive. Norman Cousins showed us that something within the body is healed when we can enjoy laughter. What is your laugh like today? Is it full and free, uninhibited as the laughter of a little child? How deep within yourself can you feel it?

The Meditation — Today I begin more actively to appreciate the opportunities for humor in life. This does not mean I take my life any less seriously or minimize the pain I have felt at various times. But from deep within myself, my body tells me clearly that laughter feels good and is an important part of my own healing. The magic of humor is another tool for healing and staying sane.

*The Affirmation — The joys around and
within my life serve as landmarks and
affirmations as to who I am today.*

The Reflection — Do you ever find yourself
thinking that the people you are meeting get
more wonderful all the time? They are more
alive, healthier and happier, more creative and
resourceful, funnier, more loving. It is probably
true that what you see in others has to do with
your own reflection in the mirror. As you feel
better about who you are, how you spend your
time and who the people are in your life, you
are able to radiate more positive energy.

The Meditation — As I move closer to wholeness, serenity and acceptance, I am attracting
people in my life consistent with this state of
mind and spiritual growth. As I examine and
change unhealthy patterns, and continue to
leave myself open to the miracle of joy, my life
will be filled with people, places and things
that can serve as landmarks of affirmation for
how far I've come.

The Affirmation — I treat my friendships as precious gems.

The Reflection — Friendships are like aspects of nature. I can take them for granted or I can make conscious decisions to appreciate their constancy, magnificence and wonder. While I certainly don't want to under-appreciate my friends or treat them insensitively, there is a healthy sense of taking for granted that simply has to do with the basic trust that my friendship is something more than whimsical and that I will not be abandoned with each unpredictable change of mood or plans.

The Meditation — Today I take a gentle inventory of who I count among my friends. I appreciate them for who they are and the gift they bring into my life. In my mind's eye I can imagine my friends to be precious gems with a unique worth all their own and collectively mirroring parts of my own journey. I embrace the trust we share — that we will not abandon each other.

The Affirmation — I will welcome the fresh breezes and blossoms of the spring season into my life.

The Reflection — There is something about spring that implies a readiness to move forward. The season comes after the cold and darkness of winter. Flowers, open air, lighter times follow. A spring mechanism bounces into a state of expansion when it is no longer confined. And winter snows melt to feed newly birthed streams. All this is simply more evidence of nature providing abundance for my needs and my pleasure.

The Meditation — I am ready for spring time. I have lived through the cold and darkness of my winter. It is now time for the hibernating seeds to push new shoots into the crisp spring air. I readily accept every flower I see as a signal of the validation I deserve. These signs are nature's reminders that it is time to spring ahead with life.

> *The Affirmation — I quiet my racing thoughts and listen as I resist the temptation to second-guess what life has in store for me.*

The Reflection — Do you remember as a child ever hearing things like "You'd better listen to me when I'm speaking to you, young man." It's that kind of intimidating, threatening message that sets up some important fears about being controlled. Losing control became equated with feeling unsafe, vulnerable and unprotected.

The Meditation — In my life today I have come to understand that to listen is to open windows and doors, to let in fresh air, new ideas. It can mean coming away with the same decisions, yet feeling more confident, more centered. In the past, listening threatened my sense of predictability, but now I know that I am not giving away any of my power or my right to decide.

---

*The Affirmation — I claim the courage
and the wisdom to follow my hunches.*

The Reflection — Sometimes, from somewhere
inside, do you have a sense that a small voice
has a message for you? Your wise inner child is
trying to tell you something about what and
how you feel. But because the intuitive part of
you has probably been squelched to the point
of near silence, the messages within you don't
have much volume to them. Yet *we* would do
well to listen with a more acutely aware ear to
what it has to say and begin making some of
the changes we've considered.

The Meditation — I begin to listen more
closely to the small voice within and recognize
the messages it has for me. In paying more
attention to these emotional road signs I can
better set my course, go in directions that are
in keeping with my highest good and invest
my energy wisely in relationships, career decisions and life events.

The Affirmation — I am awake.

The Reflection — Before recovery, I spent time either numbed out or in a state of terror that resembled a nightmare. I wasted a lot of energy as I guessed at what was true and what was my imagination. Intuition was always available to me, knocking at the walls of my need to be safe. But I was outnumbered by all those who were still playing by a set of rules that would not allow or support my expression.

The Meditation — Today I am learning to make and live by new rules. Intuition that has always been there is now free to blossom and work for me. Being awake means being alert to my experience. It means not needing to numb out. I remind myself that the moments of terror I feel today belong to the past, not to my present focus and direction. I am safe today. I can express myself and stay awake to learn from others.

The Affirmation — There is enough love, help and support to get my needs fully met in the community that surrounds me and contributes to my life.

The Reflection — How much love and support really does exist in the world? Rather than assume that there is only a limited amount available, have you ever stopped to consider that there is as much as there are people who are *willing to receive* it all? But if we continue to let our expectations about what we "deserve" to receive be governed by those old family rules we grew up with, we're likely to be disappointed.

The Meditation — In my life today I no longer have to expect sparseness or deprivation. I expand my willingness to receive, I challenge myself to succeed. I no longer have to live with a poverty consciousness. It is time to rearrange my sense of all that is available to me.

> *The Affirmation* — *I recognize my stage fright and decide to stand up and claim my life at center stage.*

The Reflection — Stage fright comes from shame — when you feel held back and weighed down by feelings of not being good enough. The fear of forgetting your lines, of missing the dress rehearsal, or of not being chosen for the right part are all self-defeating thoughts related to shame. Life doesn't take so much rehearsal. It is time- and energy-consuming.

The Meditation — Today I begin to understand that the event taking place on stage is my life. And it is my privilege to step into center stage and claim the lead role. I recognize that over-rehearsal stifles my true self. I am aware of some amount of stage fright; it tells me I am affected by what goes on. I remind myself that life truly is a stage. And as I step to the center, I leave my stage fright in the wings.

The Affirmation — I have paid my dues and deserve to claim the good harvest I have reaped.

The Reflection — When good things happen, do you find yourself thinking, "It's only a matter of time before another crisis will catch up with me"? In a house filled with inconsistency and turbulence not only did it seem you had to pay a lot of dues, you often felt the payments would have to go on forever. This kind of environment breeds an impoverished outlook on life, erodes self-worth and leaves you feeling demoralized.

The Meditation — I have gained in strength, in talents, in skills and in resources through hard work and full payment of my dues. Meeting the challenge of developing new messages means I need to make a conscious, willing effort to flex and strengthen my self-worth "muscles." But it's worth it. For I am ready to live, ready to make new marks on the slate that life offers me.

> *The Affirmation — I give myself the light, gentle touch I deserve to enhance my own healing process.*

The Reflection — The old motto that if a little bit is good, then a whole lot must be even better just doesn't work. It doesn't account for how various excesses affect you. Even in the context of recovery there are some important lessons here. Upon your initial involvement in recovery, it too can seem like the ticket to an ultimately happy life — if only you could just get enough of it. But you didn't get to where you are overnight, so go lightly.

The Meditation — With a light touch, I clear out the pieces that keep me from achieving balance. As I give myself recognition and validation for where I am today, I know that punishment, abuse and volatile treatment belong to my past. I resist the temptation to play them out in my life today, and do not allow anyone else to verbally or emotionally abuse me.

The Affirmation — I celebrate the personal power I have discovered in my life today whenever and wherever it's working toward my best interests.

The Reflection — Assertiveness is situational. No one is assertive all of the time or everywhere. Recovery does not mean learning how to act the same wonderful way all the time. Nor does it mean you have to consistently demonstrate in every situation all of those marvelous new behaviors. You'll always find some times easier to get through in your life than others.

The Meditation — Today I resist the temptation to beat myself over the head when I find it hard to use my personal power effectively. Instead I choose to recognize and celebrate those moments and situations where my personal power is actively at work for me. I have found it relatively easy to clearly express my feelings, thoughts, beliefs and ideas.

The Affirmation — I move closer to recovery each time I find my own way, each time I'm a little less lost, each time I discover a clearer sense of direction.

The Reflection — I was out walking this morning and even with the help of my trusty guide dog, managed to get briefly lost. And in the midst of trying to get my bearings to "un-lose" myself, it occurred to me that the experience may be a useful analogy for recovery. After all, isn't recovering a matter of getting back on track? Each time I find my way back from being lost, I can once again continue on my own life path.

The Meditation — As I walk today on a path that holds the promise of recovery, I know that each day brings a clearer understanding of the directions in which I need to move. I do not lose my way as often. When it seems I've gone off-track, I focus on the internal source of guidance whose true nature gracefully leads me towards my greatest good.

The Affirmation — *I choose to work hard but to love and play easy.*

The Reflection — Did you remember hearing your parents tell you something to the effect of, "Well, you're just going to have to learn this the hard way, aren't you?" In the song "The Best Of Times Is Now," there's a line that goes, "So make this moment last and live and love as hard as you know how." There's more than enough that's hard in the world. It's best to live and love as easy as you know how.

The Meditation — I begin today to reconsider what I choose to make hard in my life and what I want to be easy. I understand that remaining flexible, not trying to force things like love will bring more spontaneity into my life. Like the flowers that grow with ease under nature's gentle touch, I grant myself a richer sense of ease and enjoyment of life.

The Affirmation — I trust more fully in the experience of the natural processes of life to show me what I need to learn or do next.

The Reflection — Have you ever noticed those people in recovery who seem to cram themselves full of every resource available, always forcing themselves to emote? It's as if they've lived all their lives in a state of emotional constipation and somehow believe they can relieve themselves by using emotional laxatives. But this can be just as much a way that keeps them from getting on with life.

The Meditation — As I begin to place more trust in the natural process of life, I feel a greater sense of permission to live fully, stretching my arms wide to embrace a true passion for life, for my relationships, my activities. I cannot push the river on a journey that brings me closer and closer to my true self.

The Affirmation — I ask the universe what I need to know and quietly wait for the answers.

The Reflection — Why do we sometimes assume we know what the answers are? Or want to predict where they will or should come from? The surprise, the wondrous feeling when new answers seem to come out of nowhere is sometimes referred to as miracle. Whether you believe in miracles or not, your inner child can take the lead for developing and maintaining a posture of openness and surprise to the answers life can provide.

The Meditation — Today I know that answers can come in the form of ideas, images or passing remarks that do not seem important at first. They often come quietly or speak to us in the quiet, private places within our hearts. I look to my child within for the key, listening and knowing what is really true and what is fantasy.

The Affirmation — I enjoy laughter whenever possible, extending it outward and inviting it often into my life.

The Reflection — What messages were you given about your laughter as a child? Rather than talk about letting your child be free, start today by enjoying laughter and humor. Notice how often you have opportunities to contribute your own humor to conversations and how well it is received. Remember, the laughter you hear when you say something funny would not have happened without your involvement, creativity and contribution.

The Meditation — Today I open my heart and mind more fully to the laughter in the world. I embrace the celebration of life's good feelings in the laughter of my friends and family. A good laugh is just one outgrowth of my healing, a testimony to how far I've come, how much I can now experience all that life has, fully, passionately and without reservation.

The Affirmation — I hear with my ears and am learning to listen with my full presence.

The Reflection — Several years ago I was teaching a psychology course at a local college. Part of the course was devoted to listening skills. And it was certainly interesting to hear what some of my students thought it meant to listen to someone: "Listening means judging, agreeing and responding to what someone says." But the truth is that more than anything else, listening is a decision to focus your attention on the present moment. And in that moment, your attention communicates a great deal about your respect, concern and love.

The Meditation — Today I begin to clear my mind of the distractions that keep me from focusing on the present moment. I set aside judgments, expectations and disagreements in order to be able to listen attentively. Even when it comes to listening to myself, to the voice within, I am fully present.

*The Affirmation — I honor myself today
in my recovery by laying aside shame,
blame and impatience.*

The Reflection — The trap in working very
hard at recovery is that there's a tendency to
continue shaming and blaming ourselves and
others. It's as though it's become the "in thing"
in the recovery process to presuppose that you
and everyone else are simply full of garbage.
This is obviously not the case. None of us
deserved those traumatic events of our childhood. That we have survived and thrived is
testimony to the grace in our lives.

The Meditation — When I look back, I know
there was a time in my life when I felt tossed
aside. I did not have choices in my life as a
child. Now I do. Today I work to put aside the
shame, the blame, that edge of impatience in
my recovery. Reclaiming my life at my own pace
is a true gesture of self-love and self-respect.

> *The Affirmation — I move through my grief, using it as an important vehicle to discover my emotional freedom.*

The Reflection — I remind myself that grief and difficult emotional work are part of my journey, but do not have to be my identity or lifestyle. Grief work frees me to reclaim my own life and live fully. It helps me not to be so reactive, so tied up with a painful past and lets me be more awake in order to act. I resist the temptation to continually tell myself that I am "sick," "filled with disease," and that I will always be messed up by my past.

The Meditation — Part of my journey so far has led me through important periods of grief. I have grieved the losses, the "never hads" in my life, the pain of being violated. Grief was a vehicle to make it through to the good stuff. New doorways have been opened and I can now move forward in healing knowing more clearly where I have come from and where I now need to go.

> *The Affirmation — I step out of the trap of perfectionism and onto the platform of being my best.*

The Reflection — To be my best means I'm competing with myself to strive for betterment. I want to learn, to grow and am open to making positive changes. But the moment I get vested in doing or being anything "perfectly," I can't be satisfied with success unless I know I am always a step or miles ahead of other people. And even that won't be perfect.

The Meditation — Today as I have learned to be loving toward myself, more respectful of my own needs, I have also grown in flexibility and no longer engage the same kinds of yardsticks of self-assessment. I give up the investment in perfection that has only served to keep me from being my best. The delusion of perfection has partially robbed me of valuable self-worth. But I rebuild those foundations in my life today with my best.

The Affirmation — I empower my strength and encourage my own growth when I take small risks.

The Reflection — I have to deal a lot with the unknown on a daily basis. Consider grocery shopping, getting to work or just going for a walk to relax — without using your eyes. I have lots of help in my life to do all these things. But the point is to not lose sight of the fact that somewhere along the way *you* have to decide that it's important enough for you to find out how to get on with things in your life. You have to be willing to step into the unknown.

The Meditation — In getting on with life, I must be willing to risk stepping into places where everything is not always predictable. It means stepping into the unknown and having to learn in the moment what will make me stronger. The boost of confidence I receive when I take new risks is most growth-producing and gratifying.

> *The Affirmation — I fairly give credit to myself and to others in ways that are deserving.*

The Reflection — As children we were often not given credit for the things we did, much less for all that we endured. As adults, sometimes it is difficult to know just how far to go in giving credit to others or to ourselves for the good things we attempt and/or accomplish. Giving fair credit means having clear boundaries and a sense of integrity on which to stand.

The Meditation — Today I remind myself that giving fair credit means I am centered and free to come from a loving space within myself. I am not bogged down with resentments or the old burden of shame. Today I am free to acknowledge those things I and others have attempted and/or accomplished. I do not offer this from a place of guilt or obligation. I do not hastily give credit to others assuming this will be a safe way to ensure they will do the same for me.

The Affirmation — As I am genuinely me, I rest comfortably in my intuition for finding true genuineness in others.

The Reflection — Being genuine doesn't mean just being nice. It doesn't mean just trying to keep up that "looking good" sort of image. Being genuine doesn't mean being what others assume I am or necessarily want me to be. It doesn't mean doing what I can do to merely win the approval of others.

The Meditation — Today as an adult I pay close attention to the feelings of my own inner child. I listen to the intuitive messages about what my child wants to say or do in any given situation. I can move away from people and places where something is simply off center or uncomfortable for me. I use my adult self to take that message and find ways of expression appropriate for my life today as an adult. This does not mean playing only by the rules of others. It does mean keeping in close contact with my experience and perceptions.

> *The Affirmation — I work for myself. I work at my place of employment.*

The Reflection — How do you answer the question "Who do you work for?" Most people tell you where they work. Sometimes when things don't go well at work, you feel violated, as though you have given too much of yourself. Does your need to feel connected to others lead you to be more dedicated to your employer or company than they deserve? Perhaps it is time to remember that the time and energy you invest at work are first and foremost for *yourself.*

The Meditation — As I focus on my desires, goals, objectives and career directions, I imagine my accomplishments in light of the larger picture that is my life. While I recognize my need for being connected to others, I will use my own big picture to bolster an appropriate sense of detachment so that my work does not become my family.

The Affirmation — I am committed to the work I do and the meaning it holds for me as I remain loyal to the purposes I strive to achieve.

The Reflection — For those of us who grew up in alcoholic or other dysfunctional homes, work settings that place a premium on loyalty can be uncomfortable yet familiar. "Our happy company family" can hook us right back into the guilt, sense of fraud and vulnerability that were so much a part of our childhoods. Loyalty cannot be demanded; it can only be offered once there is a mutual foundation of trust and reasonable balance of power.

The Meditation — Today it is important to remind myself that commitment is all I need give to the place where I work. And that commitment should be no more or less than the commitment I have to my own goals and objectives. My loyalty is best reserved for my emotionally intimate relationships where the balance of power can be fairly and evenly distributed.

The Affirmation — I am observant and my observations from many different senses work for me.

The Reflection — It is one thing to be observant in a way that always keeps you just outside of living life and another to use the power of observation for the sake of learning about yourself and life. As a child you probably observed a lot: family tension, perhaps violence, dishonesty and power games. Maybe you decided many things as you observed such behavior. Consequently, observing others was a way to find out how to play the game and how to stay safe.

The Meditation — I can allow myself to be observant and spontaneous at the same time. Being observant means I remain open to my intuition. I notice my perceptions, experience and my hunches and allow myself to feel their validity. I can allow many different people to serve as role models for me, learning more about those behaviors I want as part of my lifestyle and those I do not.

The Affirmation — I take care of my inner child and do all that I can to be sure I am in a safe space wherever I am.

The Reflection — As a child you didn't always have a choice about being safe. Intuitive hunches that people and places were not always safe often had to be ignored. Perhaps you even had to talk yourself into believing you were safe merely to survive.

The Meditation — I am free to notice when I feel I am not in a safe space and to do something about it. Relationships where I am verbally, physically or sexually abused; a work setting where I am caught in power plays and dishonest communication; outright or subtle abuse in therapy — these are unsafe spaces for me. Assuming as I did as a child, "Oh it's okay, I can handle it," is only a setup for hurt and self-destructive patterns. If I need to leave an uncomfortable situation, perhaps the one who needs to most know the truth about that situation is myself.

The Affirmation — I deserve to receive.

The Reflection — Did you grow up hearing, "It is more blessed to give than to receive"? Or that you were somehow selfish and should be ashamed for wanting to receive? How do you feel today when you are given gifts or compliments? Do you get embarrassed and say to the giver, "Oh, you shouldn't have . . ." or "You didn't have to do that"? Statements such as these imply that giving to you must be a burden. Is that what you believe?

The Meditation — I will think of giving and receiving as connected in a chain. When I give, others receive. They may not give back directly to me but will undoubtedly have an opportunity to give to someone else. In turn, I may not have anything to give back directly to those who give to me but I can pass on the spirit of giving. It is by participating in and recognizing my opportunities to give that I know I too am a recipient.

111

The Affirmation — I own and actively participate in managing my inheritance.

The Reflection — My inheritance consists of all that has been passed down to me through my family line. We often speak of it in terms of money and material possessions, but it includes a host of rules, attitudes and patterns which get handed down from one generation to another.

The Meditation — As an adult I make it my business to take note of all that is in my inheritance. If I ignore what I don't wish to deal with, I run the risk of staying stuck as a victim. Managing my inheritance doesn't mean I have to keep all that has been handed down to me. Responsible management of my inheritance means staying awake and involved through the sorting process. It means looking at attitudes and behaviors which have always been and deciding which ones, if any, are best for me now.

The Affirmation — My child and adult work cooperatively together to make risk-taking a valuable part of my personal growth.

The Reflection — Risk-taking is often believed to be good for those of us involved in personal growth. My inner child may be extremely daring, waiting to get high off the next wild and crazy risks I might take. On the other hand, my child is probably timid when it comes to emotional risking. A daring child may seem open yet lack appropriate boundaries to know when risky behavior is merely an act of self-sabotage.

The Meditation — I intuitively listen to my child, giving myself time to get to know what my needs and wants are in any given situation. Needs and wants change with new situations in which I find myself, so yesterday's self-awareness may not be sufficient for today. I allow more time to truly decide what is healthy and right for me now.

The Affirmation — I have faith in a divine plan.

The Reflection — Having faith is the ability to continue walking forward even if we don't know exactly where we'll end up. Perhaps the phrase blind faith really emphasizes the kind of trust needed in the big picture of life — to know that something much bigger is going on here. With God there are no accidents. There may be plenty of circumstances we don't like or understand, but we would not be here without a definite purpose to fulfill.

The Meditation — Today I strive to set aside doubt and worry whether my journey has purpose, meaning and direction. I am willing to take just one more step beyond the limits of how far I believe I can go, trusting in the experience of how far I have already come. Although my destination may not be clear and the path poorly marked, I am reassured of an order to life that is bigger than myself which bolsters my faith along the journey.

The Affirmation — Labels in my life serve as landmarks to tell me where I am. Today I affirm who I am beyond the labels that have marked my journey.

The Reflection — Attaching our identity to a label sometimes is a useful way to know where we are, where we belong. Declaring I'm an adult child, co-dependent, alcoholic, and/or addict, is a major step towards confronting denial. But labels can also hold us back by adding to our layers of shame and blame, and by keeping us under the gun of self-punishment and self-recrimination. Labels can also be safe.

The Meditation — I remind myself that first and foremost I am a human being. I don't need to shame myself for using labels. What's important is that I allow the labels to help me deal with those things that have gotten in my way. As I take care of myself, I can get on with being the human I am beyond the labels.

> *The Affirmation — I remain centered,
> honest and calm at the core of my beliefs.*

The Reflection — It's one thing to spout off about all the things I want to think I believe; it's quite another to remain congruent and be in line with what I actually do believe. If I continually suffer from feeling I'm not getting what I want, perhaps I need to examine what I truly believe I deserve, and what I expect from life. Since I want prosperity and abundance in my life, I make a commitment to expect these results from the core of beliefs within myself.

The Meditation — I look inside to the core of my beliefs and let what I find there come into full awareness. As I honestly review my beliefs, I remain centered and seek to align the things I want in my life with the core of my self-expectations. I know and trust that the universe will only honor and respond to those things I truly believe about myself.

The Affirmation — I let fallibility serve as a signal that it's time for some humor.

The Reflection — Think of a day when you made a mistake as a small child and found it funny. Can you still tell that story and laugh about the circumstances in which you found yourself? Now imagine a time when you felt terrible about a mistake you made. What made the mistake so different from the one that was funny? Maybe the difference was merely the way you felt about yourself at the time.

The Meditation — Today I am the person most capable of putting myself at ease, the best person to give myself the approval or forgiveness I need and deserve. As I allow myself to be fallible, it becomes so much easier to soften the rigid demands I'm tempted to make of others. Owning my fallibility is not only an act of kindness to myself, it is also a gift I can offer to others that communicates a posture of caring and acceptance.

The Affirmation — My willingness to accept imperfection is a wide open door to self-forgiveness.

The Reflection — When I stay locked up in harsh judgment of myself or others and remain focused on unrelenting thoughts of perfectionism, I stay trapped in the vicious pattern of feeling ashamed. I sacrifice living in the present moment under the guise of perfection. If I don't feel okay about myself then attach a sense of being imperfect to it, I remain stuck, immobilized in a quagmire of self-pity.

The Meditation — Forgiveness is something I do first and foremost *for* myself, even when it involves forgiving someone else. I cannot forgive myself or anyone else without self-acceptance. Otherwise the result is repeating old patterns. It takes time to know and trust myself. In the face of imperfection, I can give myself this reminder and let myself and others off the relentless hook of harsh judgment.

The Affirmation — I know when I'm faking it.

The Reflection — Faking isn't always bad. It usually becomes a part of one's lifestyle from having learned that it plays an important role in survival. Perhaps it got someone off your back, kept you from failing. It worked for you or you wouldn't have done it again and again. What's important is that you don't have to confess this secret to the entire world, living the rest of your life in shame. People who notice you a lot probably already know and the shame you've felt is already more than enough for you to bear.

The Meditation — The only one who needs to know when I'm faking it is me. I am the one who deserves to know the truth and become free of the fear that has led me to fake it in the first place. I know when I am faking it and I am capable of getting the help I need to be able to live more comfortably.

> *The Affirmation — It is up to me to be fair with myself.*

The Reflection — Did you grow up being told on the one hand that "Life is not fair" and on the other that "You should always be fair"? Now that sounds unfair. The message seems to be that you're supposed to be fair to everyone else while you settle for life not being fair. Since life won't be fair and you were told you should be fair anyway, perhaps the place to begin is with yourself. After all, you're the only one getting left out of the picture.

The Meditation — When I am fair with myself, I validate my own experience and give myself permission to be fully alive, now and in the past. I have the right to make mistakes and also to have as many successes, large or small, as I can create for myself. Self-fairness means not apologizing for my abilities or talents, nor do I have to feel guilty about having opportunities in my life.

The Affirmation — I appreciate my ordinariness.

The Reflection — Arrogance is often equated with defensiveness, a sort of know-it-all attitude. Arrogance has much to do with putting ourselves down and creating unnecessary self-expectations. Assuming you have to know everything or you have to be right all the time is typical of an arrogant posture. Not only do these defensive behaviors push others away, you also end up short-changed, cheated and essentially being unfair with yourself.

The Meditation — Today I appreciate my ordinariness. It means I am only expected to do the best I can with who I am and what I have going for me. Accepting my ordinariness means I have room to learn. It means I can allow others more room to make mistakes. Letting go of arrogance means I am able to shed my fear at the pace I am willing to go.

The Affirmation — I am teachable.

The Reflection — Do you know there is no such thing as too much self-love? Statements like, "He needs to be taken down a peg or two" or "She's pretty, but the problem is she knows it" are missing a big piece of the picture. When people act as if they like themselves too much, they're still trying to like themselves at all. They overdo it in order to try to find it in the first place. Acquiring humility doesn't mean giving up self-love. Humility, the willingness to be teachable, reflects a healthy foundation of self-esteem on which to base new lessons for living.

The Meditation — I will take steps today to expand my sense of humility, to open myself up to possibilities, options and opportunities. I remind myself that humility is an active choice that sets me free to learn, to discover, to consider lessons for living that shore up the foundation for self-esteem and enhance the strength of my self-worth.

The Affirmation — I let pride work for me and not against me.

The Reflection — "Take pride in yourself . . . Don't let pride get in your way." Did you grow up hearing these messages? How do you make sense out of them today? You deserve to feel a sense of pride over your accomplishments, your skills. What gets in the way is pretending to be proud so as not to show shame or vulnerability. Using false pride as a facade is a defense that works against us, creating distance and isolation that only make it tougher to get what we want and need.

The Meditation — I look inside myself and honestly acknowledge all for which I can claim a rich, genuine sense of pride. I set aside the facade of false pride that may be borne of self-doubt, criticism and the fear that I may be "found-out." I will remind myself in moments of feeling inadequate that I own many sources of genuine pride that can work for me to honor my self-esteem.

> *The Affirmation — I trust myself and the process of life in the open spaces.*

The Reflection — What are open spaces for you? Does a lack of structure in your work or leisure time feel like too much open space? It may be similar to how you feel when you let one thing go that has been familiar, having to deal with the open space until your life is filled again by something new. Open spaces can be good times to gather internal resources. Change may abound, but inner strength and all the components that have added to your survival over the years can still go with you, working for you in creative ways.

The Meditation — Now in the open spaces, I have the opportunity to become my own self. My actions and decisions will reflect who I am as I use the vulnerability I feel as an opportunity to create meaning for myself. I decide my own course and set my own direction.

The Affirmation — I alter my expectations in order to be more in line with today, and still know I'm okay.

The Reflection — In childhood you either were good or bad. You either won or you lost when it came to competition — there was no in-between. To be good or to win meant being okay; to be bad or to lose meant you weren't. If you're still making similar demands of yourself, they are a setup for disappointment.

The Meditation — When I alter my expectations, I have more room to breathe. Without such an old rigid agenda about what I must achieve, I create the freedom to accomplish things and still enjoy myself. As I remain flexible and open to new options, I can expand the sources that contribute to my sense of being worthwhile, capable and competent. Seeing things only in black and white creates tunnel vision and blinds me to the vast areas that lie in between "either/or" thinking.

> *The Affirmation — Pain and frustration are signals for the permission to make needed changes in my life.*

The Reflection — When in the midst of pain and challenging times, it is so tempting to wish the universe would suddenly change strategies and deal a fair deck, a kinder hand in my direction. All too often I fall into the trap of thinking I have to wait my turn. On the contrary, the pain and frustration I feel are signaling it's time to make some changes — time to call my life as I see it and make sure my needs are being met.

The Meditation — I will ensure that my needs are met. I know this has more to do with how determined and/or aggressive I am with my own self-honesty than with any demands I make on others. I am aware I can choose not to act on the signals of change that pain and frustration cause in my life, but I cannot ignore their presence. Any action towards positive change I take will be at my own pace, in my own time.

> *The Affirmation — I have enough to do
> just taking one step at a time.*

The Reflection — It is so easy, so tempting to try
to project the future — trying to plan all the
things that need to be done, to make sure
everything I want to accomplish actually gets
done. Often, with too much projection, I'll
begin to feel overwhelmed, overburdened and
exhausted. Life has such a way of surprising me
with opportunities and obstacles that it is a
waste of energy to plan far ahead. But by just
taking one step at a time, I find the universe also
comes through with a wealth of the resources I
need, often exactly when I need them.

The Meditation — Today I choose to let go of
my efforts to control, predict and project the
entire picture of my future. I will use my visions of the future as sources of inspiration for
what I hope to accomplish. Yet I know I need
to focus primarily on the one step ahead of me
just now.

> *The Affirmation — I have the complete rights to my own integrity.*

The Reflection — While adulthood is not the pure recreation of childhood, it has certain benefits to which we are fully entitled. Integrity is one of them. It has to do with a basic sense of worth and it begins within ourselves. To be treated as though you have integrity means that the positive way you feel about yourself is no mystery, no secret to others. Your integrity belongs to you and projects the image of all that you have survived and the foundation you have built at the core of your self-worth.

The Meditation — Today I stand for all to see on the rock of my integrity. I am free to proclaim my self-worth without arrogance or false pride through my inheritance as a human being. I wear my self-esteem with grace and let others know they have earned theirs as much as I've earned mine.

The Affirmation — I appreciate my own accomplishments and use them to build the foundation of my self-confidence.

The Reflection — What I'm able to accomplish is based on what I was able to do yesterday. It's so easy to add up my weaknesses, to sell myself short over mistakes I have made. All too often I forget to appreciate just how far I have come, the changes I've made, the ways I express myself differently within relationships and in reflecting on my own internal experience of the world.

The Meditation — Each and every gain I make comes out of work I have done. Sometimes it is subtle, taking place slowly over time. My changes come in small and in large steps. I have needed to observe life, to ask questions, to try on new behaviors and take some risks. As I look toward the future and my own individual goals, I give myself the confidence I deserve by remembering how far I have come.

The Affirmation — I make choices and accept the mothering that is good for me today.

The Reflection — I find in living with blindness that a lot of people have tried to mother me. Some of the mothering I've received has helped to further set me free and remove barriers while other forms have only served to smother me, nearly choking my own well-developed capabilities. So I have to be selective about the mothering I accept. While I have no wish to be smothered, I also don't want to inadvertently throw all of their efforts away.

The Meditation — As an adult, I decide about what is appropriate mothering for me and what is not, based on my needs now. The bottom line is that I am my own parent. I can reject the well-intended offerings of others who may be getting their own needs met instead of being tuned into mine. I keep those pieces that work for me and put aside those which do not help me move forward.

The Affirmation — I am open to the excitement of discovery.

The Reflection — Sometimes when people become involved in the journey of personal growth, they become self-critical and skeptical, assuming that everything they discover about themselves will or should be negative. Yet discovery can be a wonderful experience. Think of the people you've met, seemingly by chance, through other people you know. Remember some of the opportunities you've found just by being in the right place at the right time.

The Meditation — In my life I am continuing on a journey filled with discovery — about myself and about human nature. Along the way I will no doubt find some things about myself I do not like or wish had never happened. But even in those there are essential lessons for living. Everything I discover about myself has value and I will cherish the excitement of the discovery process.

The Affirmation — *I greet today with a sense of gladness.*

The Reflection — I have the right and the freedom to greet each new day with gladness. Each day my life is more my own as I claim my rights, resources and responsibilities. I deserve all the pure and genuine joy I can create or that comes across my path. Gladness is something I express in friendliness. It comes through my appearance and my ability to respond to life flexibly, assertively and confidently. Gladness comes through my laughter, my tone of voice and my body language. It's contagious and accumulates interest in my personal psychological bank account.

The Meditation — I welcome the day with a sense of gladness, knowing I deserve brightness where too much darkness has shrouded my life. I extend a joyful invitation to the universe and others to celebrate the contagious process of gladness with open arms and hearts of freedom.

The Affirmation — I keep my appointment today.

The Reflection — Whether we're talking about a tangible arrangement, such as a visit to a therapist or doctor or referring to purpose in life, an appointment is an agreement to be somewhere at a particular time. The appointment is the commitment that "I will show up. I will be present." If you lacked a healthy role model who could demonstrate what it means to make and keep commitments, it may have become tempting very early to wiggle out of plans and life purpose.

The Meditation — Today I know my time is not to be wasted. I agree with myself to use it wisely. I agree to make and keep appointments in a responsible way. As I grow through my journey, I gain a clearer vision of the directions and purposes towards which I am working. I remind myself that the first appointment I need to keep is with myself.

The Affirmation — Every day I am un-covering the buried treasure of myself and my life.

The Reflection — All too often the process of recovery can feel burdensome. Somehow the old shaming voices of the past still make their presence known and lead us to undeserved self-criticism and unnecessary harsh judgment. But recovery means reclaiming. It means getting back those treasures that were temporarily lost. The pain that is felt in the process is a mere part of the journey. It is a doorway, a threshold over which we must cross. Pain is in no way meant to be the new way of life.

The Meditation — It's time to uncover buried treasure — talents, dreams, the ability to enjoy playfulness and closeness. It's time to uncover memories that reaffirm all that I've survived. Even though I know I must step over thresholds of pain, there are treasures yet to be uncovered in my life that lie just beyond the doorways from the past.

The Affirmation — My keys are always with me and within me.

The Reflection — Somewhere along the way we usually learn that it pays to be responsible about where we put our keys — house key, car key, the key to the office, etc. Not being able to locate the right key when necessary can produce inconvenient consequences and situations. This is as true for the intangible keys, such as our own internal resources.

The Meditation — The keys I need are right within me — the skills for handling my work, my personal growth, my relationships. They include my intuition and my hunches about what is going on beyond what is apparent. At the beginning of each day or at the start of a challenging experience, I take stock of the keys I have right within me. They can be as intense as the ability to think on my feet in order to get out of a potentially dangerous situation, and as light as the timing of spontaneous humor.

> *The Affirmation — I am enjoying the earth and all the abundance nature offers.*

The Reflection — Enjoying the earth is a wonderful way to enhance our spiritual connections to ourself and the world. Smelling flowers, noticing the sun, feeling the rainfall, going for a walk in the woods, eating fresh fruits and vegetables are ways to tap into the intricacies and appreciate the miracle of how life is put together. There is little doubt that there has been some planning of nature that is far bigger than you or I can.

The Meditation — Today I pay tribute to the earth. I appreciate the way nature constantly supplies me with abundance. I notice what I take in through my senses with full awareness and take time to quietly honor all the magnificence. I allow myself to find personal meaning and definition in nature's presence and splendor.

> *The Affirmation — I pause and re-member the people, relationships and ex-periences that have been my "teachers" on life's path.*

The Reflection — Consider how often you're tempted to view people and things as fitting into stereotyped rigid categories. Children are to be children, to be approached as little people who know less. Animals are to be taken care of and trained. As long as there are those who are to be taught, then there are those who are only supposed to do the teaching. When people stay tucked neatly inside their own set roles, there is no flexibility and little learning takes place.

The Meditation — Today I notice a host of things I have learned from people, events and experiences. I learn by the example that others set, allowing them to be role models for me. I can learn what I don't want in my life as well as more of what I do want. I am open to learning much in the way of insight and trust in my intuition.

---

*The Affirmation — I find my own way
to relax today.*

The Reflection — When anyone told me to
relax as a child, it usually meant they were
about to do something to me I didn't want.
What memories do you have as a child around
the word relax? Was it your parents' way of
telling you to calm down, that you were getting
too wound up? Such messages restrict and con-
strain the full spectrum of our emotional responses and we're left with a narrow range of
"acceptable" feelings.

The Meditation — Today I find a quiet place
inside where no one can violate or disturb me.
I allow the word relax to take on a new meaning. I put on hold all those busy thoughts that
keep me buzzing and know they will be there
later when I want them. I quiet any fear and
gently remind myself that I relax in my own
time, at my own pace, in a safe place where I
can stay attuned to my own center and remain
aware of my own needs.

> *The Affirmation — I am the center of my universe.*

The Reflection — Were you raised to believe that it's wrong to be selfish? If so, then you might tend to believe that people who say they are at the center of their universe are self-centered and egotistical. Your universe consists of all of the circumstances in your life, your activities, relationships and decisions you've made over the years. It includes your perceptions, thoughts, feelings and your intuition. In fact, there is no one more important in your universe than you, so you need to know what being at the center of your own life truly means.

The Meditation — Being at the center of my universe means assessing what's really important to me. I recognize the important differences between it and self-centeredness. Being at the center of my universe means deciding what is best for me and assuming the responsibility for my actions, attitudes and achievements.

---

*The Affirmation — I let the rainbow of
people in the universe help to expand my
vision.*

The Reflection — When you see a rainbow, do
you believe it can bring you good luck? That
sense of magic that comes from rainbows may
hold lessons about your feelings and perceptions of the variety of people and all of our
human differences. We can be so myopic and
tunnel-visioned about other people's lifestyles.
When someone lives differently from what you
believe is correct, you may simply decide they're
living the wrong way.

The Meditation — I let my awareness of the
rainbow of differences give me more permission to decide what is right for me. In turn I am
more free to let others be who they are and
make their own decisions. I and my lifestyle are
as much a part of the rainbow of people as the
next person. And the spectrum we all create
together is a testimony to the magic of differences in a world filled with rainbows.

The Affirmation — I exercise the right to set boundaries on my needs for privacy.

The Reflection — Perhaps some of the disturbing memories many of us have involve violations of privacy — some form of sexual exploitation, being humiliated by parents or teachers, having others assume they know better about our needs and make choices for us or help themselves to our personal belongings. These memories can serve as reference points to help establish more clearly your boundaries today.

The Meditation — The whispers and screams of my inner child tell me it's time to exercise the rights to set some boundaries, especially on my personal privacy. Perhaps I have been so used to acquiescing to others that I assume they know what's best for me. It is not true for me now. No one knows my internal signals like I do, and no one can set and maintain my privacy boundaries better than I.

The Affirmation — I listen to the messages of my spirit both within and throughout my life.

The Reflection — What is the essence of the messages that guide and inspire our lives? Our spirit reflects the feelings, content, context and definitions embedded in our lives. All of these can yield intuitive clues and cues in our search for guidance, direction and meaning in the daily process of living.

The Meditation — The moods, reactions and tendencies of my child within deserve to be noticed. I pay attention to the definite and more subtle responses to others in my life. These serve as reflections I can use to build spiritual strength and seek meaning. As I focus my attention on all of the messages of my spirit, I am reminded that guidance comes from a place that lives within me and permeates throughout my life.

> *The Affirmation — I treasure my body as nature's own.*

The Reflection — With all of the pressure from the media, fashion, fad and internalized messages from the past, what is it like for you to be inside your body today? Do you find yourself still feeling like a little child inside, trying to figure out this adult-sized body you're carrying around? One part of you fully understands what it means to feel vulnerable, yet this has to be reconciled with being a grown-up who has to get on with life.

The Meditation — Today I know that my body needs and deserves a well-spring of love from within myself and from others to help heal any sense of shame about not being okay. Nurturance revitalizes my body's sense of wellness as I remain attentive and in tune with myself. My adult-sized body carries every aspect of who I am, including my inner child. I nurture my body, being wise to stay away from violation of any kind.

The Affirmation — I respect my dreams and pay attention to the lessons that emanate from my unconscious.

The Reflection — Just think about how many creative ideas have come to fruition that began as the lingering recollections from a night's sleep. Yet how often are daydreams and fantasies discouraged and nighttime dreams laughed off and forgotten? All of these mental creations are windows to the unconscious, portals through which we can see into the mind's eye and become consciously aware of our conflicts, needs, solutions and creative ideas.

The Meditation — I embrace the lessons of dreams. They work for me, giving me outlets to express and understand my fears, desires and doubts. I may have been told as a child that too much daydreaming was not the responsible thing to do. Today I know that my daydreams, fantasies and nighttime dreams are friends that work for me as I work with them.

> *The Affirmation — I respect my curiosity
> and act upon it with integrity.*

The Reflection — Did your parents ever tell you
that "curiosity killed the cat" when they thought
you were being too curious for your own good?
Do you think what they really meant was too
curious for their good? Or too curious because
nobody wanted to answer your questions?
Maybe they didn't even have the answers. Curiosity is a basic drive to want to *know.* As we
grow and can couple knowledge with discern-
ment and good judgment, we develop wisdom.

The Meditation — Today I appreciate and
wisely use my curiosity. When I am tempted to
be curious about things that don't concern me,
I consider the possibility that I am seeking a
way to deal with my anger toward someone, or
simply wanting some attention and recognition.
I put aside such temptations, knowing I can
learn from them without acting upon them.

> *The Affirmation — I take the pressure
> off myself and simply speak honestly for
> myself from the reality I know best.*

The Reflection — Most people who have been
involved in personal growth, therapy or communication education have heard about the
importance of "I" statements. Not only does
this rapport-building strategy create an environment where others feel emotionally safe, it
also gives us a true sense of freedom. Speaking
for ourselves puts the responsibility on each of
us to be honest. We take the pressure off ourselves and relieve the assumption that we need
to know anything concrete about the reality of
anyone other than ourselves.

The Meditation — Today I take the pressure off
myself by resolving to simply say what is true
for me. I cannot read minds in order to know
about other peoples' feelings or thoughts, nor
will I accept this expectation from them. Today,
speaking honestly for myself creates new freedom in my life.

The Affirmation — *The mistakes of others provide me with a model for changes in my own life.*

The Reflection — It's so easy to be critical. Often we expect those with degrees, good looks, fame, money or any sort of expertise to "have it all together." When they don't act consistently with this image, we are prone to discredit them. It's as if we believe that now there is little or nothing to be learned from them. But the opposite is actually true. We can use the mistakes of others as role models for creating changes in our own lives.

The Meditation — Today I reflect on my thoughts of others, noticing particularly where I have been critical, angry and disappointed. I remember that they are human too. They are pioneers, just as I am a pioneer in my own life. Many people will cross my path and teach me. I use my disappointment to make changes, knowing that blaming others can be yet another way of distracting myself from my own growth.

The Affirmation — I accept the freedom to discriminate in choosing who I let into my life and who I do not.

The Reflection — Setting boundaries is crucial to emotional health. Without clear boundaries, our time is not our own, our bodies don't belong to us, our thoughts and values remain diffuse and cloudy. The next step is learning to maintain those boundaries through a process of active choice. Not only must we choose who will come in or out of our lives, more subtle distinctions must also be made, such as, how close, how long, how intimate do we want to become.

The Meditation — Today I am clear that not everyone who reaches out to me will have a place in my life. I know there are people who are not good for me; their reach, intentional or not, is more of an invasion than an invitation. I remind myself that setting boundaries doesn't mean keeping everyone out. I give myself the freedom to make choices.

> *The Affirmation — My adult-size body
> reminds me of all that I have survived.*

The Reflection — The situations and events that can trigger recollections of being a fairly vulnerable little child sometimes surprise you. Once I almost accepted a job that just didn't feel right. In describing the interview experience to a friend, I said, "It's this place with BIG hallways . . . BIG offices with lots of people." My friend and I went on to exaggerate the setting with how there were all these BIG desks, BIG people, and then there was *little* me.

The Meditation — I didn't get to be an adult without having solved all sorts of challenges over the years. Certainly that little child inside me feels vulnerable, particularly in new situations. I do not need to ignore this little person, nor possess superhuman strength. I can draw faith from the survival reflected in my adult-sized body to remind myself of getting beyond uncertainty.

The Affirmation — I simplify my life by accepting feelings and facts for just what they are.

The Reflection — Feelings aren't right or wrong; they simply exist. Facts are just facts. They can refer to the reality of a situation such as someone's opinion. Perhaps the feelings you and I have are part of the facts about a circumstance in which we find ourselves. This also means that the feelings, opinions and thoughts of others are just as much a part of the facts in any situation.

The Meditation — I accept feelings and facts as part of reality. The facts of a situation are simply the circumstances as they are. Choosing to ignore them, to attempt to change them without acceptance only complicates my life. I make great strides in my life by recognizing the simplicity of things as they are. I was unable to accept things as simply in the past because I needed to protect my shaky self-esteem with my defenses.

> *The Affirmation — I greet this day wide-eyed, open to all the surprises and wonder it holds.*

The Reflection — Do you wake up expecting each day to be merely a carbon copy of the many days gone before? Or do you wake up with a sense of optimism and expectancy? Do you remember the wide-eyed sort of curiosity you might have had as a child? Consider looking into your mind's eye to keep that sense of wonder a part of your daily experience now.

The Meditation — Today as I reach out to grow, I am again amazed at all that I find — undiscovered gifts, underused resources, yet-to-be-developed talents — waiting to be claimed right within me. I allow my enthusiastic child within to work for me in bringing about the expectancy and joy of surprise. I let myself greet this day and all that is before me with wide-eyed inner vision and an outer expression that reaffirms the wonder of discovering the world that surrounds me and the spirit that lives within.

> *The Affirmation — I find renewed vital-*
> *ity and joy as I allow my childlike spirit to*
> *be expressed.*

The Reflection — There is a difference between being childish and childlike. Childishness tends to be all the negative behaviors we don't want to see exhibited, even in children: whining, tantrums, irresponsibility of any kind. Child-likeness, on the other hand, is the word for the most ideal attributes of children. The ideals associated with it can be creatively applied to our adulthoods today.

The Meditation — With open arms I embrace the childlike spirit within me. My playfulness, sense of humor, even my capacity for silliness, add to my personality and restore sanity. I cannot recreate my childhood. But I can let my childlike spirit be a daily part of my friendships, intimate relationships and spiritual growth. I can see through childlike eyes into the truly valuable person I am today.

> *The Affirmation — I say hurray for playfulness!*

The Reflection — We hear a lot about adult children having trouble with playfulness. Perhaps that becomes true when there is too much analysis, too much sense that someone is watching and grading us. Whether playfulness is a regular part of our past experience or not, there is always room for it to be a part of our lives today.

The Meditation — I let my playfulness be a part of my expression and interaction with others today. Playfulness can add to so many aspects of my life — relationships, ideas, self-esteem, intimacy. I can tease others in a loving way and enjoy being teased in return. I can play with animals and with children. What's important is that I know the door to my playfulness is there, waiting to be opened. I can also close it when I need to be serious or quiet. But even when busy with work and the responsibilities of adulthood, I can let my sense of playfulness come through and express itself.

The Affirmation — I trust spontaneity to add to my life.

The Reflection — Many of us are confused between being spontaneous and acting compulsively. If large portions of your childhood were chaotic, it may be hard to accept spontaneity as a positive element in your life now. But spontaneity is part of being childlike. It exists in degrees; it doesn't have to be all or nothing. I know I am risking when I dare to be spontaneous, and taking risks is usually best done a step at a time. What I've found in many ways is that being spontaneous has a lot to do with giving up my rehearsal and tendency to be calculating.

The Meditation — As I make room to accept spontaneity as a part of my life, I remind myself that living spontaneously is something more than merely letting my impulses run wild. I have been accumulating a growing sense of who I am and of my own internal resources. My childlike spontaneity is something based on a growing foundation of who I am today.

The Affirmation — I am free to allow only safe touch of my physical body.

The Reflection — Most of us would not simply stand around and let anyone physically abuse us. Yet often in relationships where loyalty and low self-worth come into play, abuse can be commonplace. But what of behavior that isn't necessarily abusive but you just don't like, such as nudges, pats and touches in places and in ways that take unfair advantage of your emotional vulnerability? Physical touch can then feel unsafe, threatening or violating.

The Meditation — I make it my business to get the safe touch I need. One significant outcome of my personal growth is that I am becoming more awake to those moments when the touch I'm receiving doesn't feel safe. I'm faster at perceiving those subtle moments when I'm feeling violated. More quickly and easily, I'm able to remove myself from the unpleasantness and change the circumstances.

> *The Affirmation* — I let my feelings of
> *lust work for me.*

The Reflection — Many of us grew up learning
that lust is unhealthy, dangerous or shameful.
Recovery groups of various kinds dealing with
sex addiction or love and relationship addiction
are testimony to the struggles we've had with
this. Typically we've vacillated between being
rigidly good or rebelliously bad. What's been
missing is a sense of peace in living with
sexual attraction, the desire for intimacy and
self-esteem to allow it to happen.

The Meditation — I allow my feelings of lust to
tell me more about who I am and what I want
or need. I do not shame myself for sexual
attractions or fantasies. I turn off the replays of
old tapes where I have ceaselessly punished
myself for past mistakes and allow myself to
move in the present with wisdom and integrity.
I recognize that feelings of lust are a mere form
of energy. These desires and fantasies affirm
my aliveness, my zeal and potency.

156

The Affirmation — I am learning to trust myself.

The Reflection — With so much information available and different ways to live and perceive our experience, it is sometimes difficult to know what is "really" the truth, which road is the right one to take. But if all of the answers were meant to be summed up in one or two simplistic packages, we wouldn't have a whole lifetime given to us to figure it out. The process is one of gradual unfolding, awareness and ability to appreciate the subtle.

The Meditation — I stop all the noise in my head and remember how often things have worked out exactly as they were meant to, in spite of how complicated I made them. Forever analyzing and hanging on to a need for control only divides me from my sense of self. I ask the Universe to tell me what I need to know. As I get out of my way and loosen my grip on controlling the events around me, I'm amazed at how much more energy I have to enjoy life.

The Affirmation — I know the physical and emotional differences between hugging and being held, and I give myself the choice that's most comfortable.

The Reflection — There's a difference between hugging and holding. When we hug, we're usually still on our feet, perhaps somewhat on guard or controlled. It can be a gesture that keeps everyone safe but not necessarily able to connect. Being held or holding someone expresses more vulnerability. There's no need to be on your feet, guess at what's safe or keep your distance. You can be quiet or highly expressive.

The Meditation — I listen carefully to my needs for closeness. I become increasingly honest and selective about when I want to be hugged or when I want to be held. Likewise, I am also clearer about when I want to be left alone. I let my body language work for me in creating the distance or the closeness I want.

The Affirmation — Taking care of myself is a fulltime job.

The Reflection — Aren't there a bunch of things in life that, once we've taken care of them, we'd like to believe are finished, done? But taking care of ourselves means staying current in relationships where there is any sort of commitment to clear communication. It means taking care of health, exercise, rest and nutrition. Taking care of ourselves means continuing to grow and nurture ourselves with whatever spiritual meaning we can sustain.

The Meditation — Today, taking care of myself is a fulltime job. It doesn't have to be a serious burden, but it does deserve my full attentiveness. It means I respect myself enough to stay current with the awareness of my needs, wants and experience. I do not hope that whatever I did for myself six months ago will be enough to live on for the next year. I expect and deserve a conscious commitment to quality self-care.

The Affirmation — I feel the loss and the presence of my father in my present life circumstances. I acknowledge and embrace his presence when I am aware of it.

The Reflection — Five years after my father died, I finally was dealing with the grief in therapy. I hadn't been aware of missing him on a daily basis through much of my life, so it was hard to grieve until I got back in touch with key events, recollections and moments that exposed my vulnerability. But now there are also many moments when I can connect with some important components of nurturance, playfulness and other qualities that soothe the missing pieces.

The Meditation — I acknowledge that my experience with my father had certain feelings of loss inherent in our time together. While I cannot recreate my childhood, I know that as I walk through and emerge from the grief of losses, I can embrace and incorporate a new sense of healing. That reconnects me solidly with the love I've missed.

The Affirmation — In the joy of my self-discovery I experience a continuous flow of renewal.

The Reflection — Do you remember the feeling of joy when you got something new as a child — new shoes, new clothes, new toys? Maybe these were times of feeling a sense of renewal, new beginning, new hope. With a little imagination you might also notice how "renew" sounds just like "re-knew." It's as if life were a spiral. While we may once again find ourselves in the midst of sorting out old issues that have resurfaced, we somehow "re-know" what we need to do.

The Meditation — Today I carry the childlike spirit and the adult wisdom into a sense of renewal. I can greet my new life, my new sense of self with a feeling of joy and positive expectancy. I know that renewal for me today is not based on escape. It is based on growing faith, an expanded sense of appreciation for myself and full recognition that it's okay to celebrate myself.

The Affirmation — *I respect boundaries that exist beyond the physical body.*

The Reflection — When I find that someone has been petting my guide dog without my permission or knowledge, I feel invaded. That so many people think nothing of petting a strange dog, much less one that is working, without even asking, reflects a boundary problem in our culture. Of course she's cute. But think about what might happen if people took the same sort of license with a friend walking beside you.

The Meditation — Where do my boundaries begin and end? Are there ways in which I am tired of being invaded by others? Perhaps I have continually allowed something to go on that I assume is considered normal by others but is an invasion to me. I listen to and respect where my boundaries begin and end. I use this information to take better care of myself and to read and respect the messages of others as they learn about and express their own boundaries.

The Affirmation — When I say no adamantly, it's a signal for me to look at my fear.

The Reflection — Sometimes I can get into "The No Mo." The expression stands for "The No Modality." It reminds me to back away from my one-track mindedness. It's a vital part of personal growth. On the other hand, when an adamant no leaves no room for mutual expression, then there is a threat to self-esteem, to personal survival. It is replaying an old scenario where a tantrum or other survival response seemed to be the only way to retain a sense of personal autonomy.

The Meditation — When I'm in the "No Mo," I realize that there may be an element of truth in what I'm hearing. The intensity of my no is a clue to just how much I don't want to hear or recognize this. Even though I don't want to feel vulnerable, I consider the element of truth presented and know that I need not be threatened by this. I place the experience on hold until I can explore it safely.

> *The Affirmation — I take a vacation from working on myself so hard.*

The Reflection — Lots of people talk about recovery as an attitude towards life and the daily process of living, yet so many people would lead you to believe that you have to read so many books, attend so many meetings a week, and oh, yes, don't forget to make your amends and count your blessings, etc. There's no dress rehearsal for life or recovery. Live both today. Don't save all the good stuff until you think you've got it right.

The Meditation — I give myself a well-earned vacation from working so hard on myself. My personal growth goals and commitment to recovery are both strong. Yet I come to realize it is important to set my own pace and get where I need to go in the time it's going to take. I cannot chase recovery, nor can I push it along and hurry it any faster. I will take the opportunity to enjoy living, celebrate my recovery and take vacations when I need to do that.

> *The Affirmation* — *I listen to and respect my timetable in dealing with my emotions.*

The Reflection — In this era of recovery/personal growth, we run the risk of having just as much peer pressure and programming as we have had with the generation before us. When all our friends are talking in personal growth jargon or going off to treatment to get "fixed," there may be this sense that "I *should* be doing what they're doing" or "I need someone to tell me what's really going on with me, too."

The Meditation — I step back from all the furor of what I read and hear to pay close attention to my own awareness. As a child I may have learned there wasn't time to make careful, deliberate decisions, to respect my own emotional process. I may have learned to hurriedly make safe decisions that wouldn't rock the boat. Ultimately, the pressure I feel in recovery may be doing me the favor of respecting and listening to the ticking of my internal clock of change and growth.

> *The Affirmation — I am able to see beyond the superficial pleasures of instant gratification.*

The Reflection — Junk food, crummy living conditions, crumbly relationships — all of these can be had instantaneously. In the absence of true contact with other people or a sense of real meaning, these may look appealing: something sweet and fun to eat, someone with charm and promises, a quick financial deal that *sounds* foolproof and exciting. Yet something that looks enticing on the surface may wreak havoc on our bodies and our spirits.

The Meditation — Today I take a moment to myself to quietly move beyond the initial excitement of any quick deals I hear about. I do not have to rush. I know the good that is really right for me will not vanish. I need time to get beyond the deceptiveness of being enticed by outer circumstances that only seem harmless in disguise.

The Affirmation — I am entitled to express and seek fulfillment of my unmet needs.

The Reflection — A friend once asked me how I was. I answered, "I'm fine, except that I'm walking around with so many unmet needs." We laughed at the time, both rather surprised by such a bold statement and made a lot of jokes about unmet needs after that incident. What we realized later was how much of the silence and secrecy about carrying these unmet needs around was relieved.

The Meditation — What unmet needs am I living with today? I ask myself and listen for my own answers. What needs might be buried just below the surface for fear of being rejected, criticized or misunderstood? Just as I would respect the needs of anyone I care about, I respect my own now. Today I know that becoming freer through personal growth means taking the courage to express my unmet needs with those who I can trust.

> *The Affirmation — I create clear boundaries for myself.*

The Reflection — As part of an exercise in therapy to clarify boundaries in relationships, I came up with three categories of friends — bedroom friends, living-room friends and front porch friends. Bedroom friends were people with whom I could feel safe and emotionally vulnerable. Living-room friends were important social relationships but with less emotional closeness. Front porch friends were merely acquaintances. When I'm uncertain about the direction I want to take in a relationship, I use this exercise and imagine the room in which I can most easily envision this person.

The Meditation — I think about those with whom I spend time and notice how I feel as I reflect on each. With some people I want to be closer, with others I want more distance. Tools like the metaphor of rooms guide me to my feelings, help clarify boundaries and empower my choice-making process.

The Affirmation — *I appreciate the many options I have and do what I can to find the information required to exercise my choices.*

The Reflection — Living life as a victim often feels like living without options. When you feel this way, brainstorm some options and develop a plan of action. Verbally or in writing, list all the possibilities you can imagine. Don't censure any ideas that come to mind. Once you have a list, scrutinize each choice carefully, weigh pros and cons. Once you identify a choice that appeals to you, ask yourself what resources you'll need to make that change. Chances are it will have something to do with finding some needed information and direction.

The Meditation — Today I move forward to claim a strengthened sense of choice and possibility in my life. Even though as a child I perceived few choices and poor possibilities, I have grown beyond the victim's posture.

The Affirmation — I use my recovery to get on with life.

The Reflection — Some people can turn anything into a rigid lifestyle or a form of personal identity with as many rules and regulations as the dysfunctional families they grew up in. Consider how some people will use their "status" and involvement in recovery to rigidly proclaim that other recovering people are the only ones worthy of honest communication. And simultaneously make sweeping, pejorative generalizations about "outsiders."

The Meditation — Today I remind myself that a critical purpose of personal growth and recovery is to improve the quality of my life and all my relationships. How able and willing I am to communicate with people in my daily life is a true measure of progress, whether the gains have been made from therapy or groups. Regardless of the source, I seek to use all the tools of recovery with finesse to get on with my life.

> *The Affirmation* — *I do not have to take the world the way it's handed to me.*

The Reflection — To know we have choices helps us keep a certain sense of freedom in life. But this was not always the case. As a child I was told to eat what was put in front of me. That message carried over into other expectations about me. The translation: "Take the world the way it was handed to you." But sometimes the way the world dishes out life to us is simply not in our best interests.

The Meditation — Today I know that the responsibility for my life is with me. I have the power to make choices and set aside whatever guilt I may feel about changing my mind. I respect the courage it takes to realize that something is just not for me — a new job, a relationship, a task I agreed to do. I need to take risks to follow through with this discovery. But it also brings me the clarity, freedom and honesty required for future decisions.

> *The Affirmation — From life experience,
> a foundation of continuity has emerged
> that I can now use to anchor myself.*

The Reflection — Even within the personal growth movement, there have been numerous fads that have come and gone. While trying new ideas can be exciting and beneficial, well-intentioned peer pressure and other persuasions may convince you to try something, indulge in some newfangled experience that just isn't you, that only serves to make you uncomfortable. These can leave you feeling like you're just not "with it."

The Meditation — Today I take the time to feel grounded in a sense of continuity about my life. I can choose to open myself up to new ideas without discrediting or discounting the ways I've worked on myself in the past. I remember that I am *not* a beginner. I have worked hard and have survived well. I trust the accuracy of my intuition and the foundation of my own life experiences.

The Affirmation — I choose self-under-standing as my life's project built on the full range of my experiences.

The Reflection — Of all the things to do in life — have a family, build a career, achieve goals and aspirations — what is more important than self-understanding? While there are books and tapes, workshops and therapy, true self-under-standing comes through life experience. It comes through becoming aware of my reactions, my attractions. It comes through finding the courage to *feel my feelings*, not just think them.

The Meditation — I center my attention on my own personal growth and ask myself what else I can learn from the circumstances I'm in right now. What mirrors can I find in my reactions toward other people? What can I learn about my frustrations, or my sense of joy? I have work to do, and my own self-understanding is a major key in fulfilling my life purpose.

---

*The Affirmation — I put aside the temp-
tation to use Band-Aids to cope and am
willing to change.*

The Reflection — Coping is sometimes essential to survival. We may have found in childhood that our role models depended upon
coping mechanisms — taking tranquilizers,
drinking regularly, remaining defensive, using
any behavior to take away pain or threat. Yet as
old pain continues to return in various life
situations, it becomes more difficult, if we are
honest, to believe that the old coping strategies
are working.

The Meditation — I am willing to change. My
reading this book is a sign that I am committed
to improving the quality of my life. I don't have
to make any new behavior a part of my life
forever. I can just decide to be willing to do just
one thing differently. Whatever the changes are,
I decide to try the ones that are in my best
interest, knowing that the best changes take
place slowly and need to feel right on the inside.

The Affirmation — I have faith beyond mere endurance as I envision the big picture.

The Reflection — Endurance is similar to tolerance — both imply a certain amount of passivity, both suggest living one's life without much of a sense of inspiration. A certain amount of acceptance is inherent in both. But to have faith beyond endurance suggests that we not only see the larger picture in life, but that the details are not that important. At some level we simply know we are going to get where we want to go, assume a certain amount of divine trust and proceed.

The Meditation — I work moment by moment towards the full experience of faith beyond endurance. It's okay to not know exactly how to do this, but I trust it is part of my spiritual development in life. Faith beyond endurance takes me into a life where I can continue breathing, continue living, trust that life is good and that I deserve the best it has to offer.

The Affirmation — In detachment I re-mind myself of who I am.

The Reflection — Detachment sometimes sounds cold and heartless. On the contrary, it is one of the warmest and fastest tools for re-energizing ourselves once we've got going. Detachment really means giving the power back to ourselves. Detaching is removing our-selves from situations long enough to get refo-cused and to draw upon our sense of em-powerment. The process is similar to what many personal growth guides teach as center-ing and grounding exercises.

The Meditation — Today I remind myself that any difficult relationships or situations do not own me. While I may be frustrated with cir-cumstances, I do not need to become so en-meshed with them that I fail to see the big picture. I remind myself that I am not all that these circumstances remind me of, that there is a great deal more to who I am and who I will yet become.

The Affirmation — It's okay to change my mind.

The Reflection — One day in therapy, after gaining a new perspective on something, I felt very relieved in saying to my therapist, "I'm so glad it's all right with you if I change my mind." She chuckled and said, "Changing your mind is the purpose of this therapy." In my alcoholic home, changing my mind was a sign that I was behaving like my irresponsible father. Holding steadfast to decisions was a sign of "maturity."

The Meditation — In allowing myself to change my mind today, I am more in touch with myself in the moment. I recognize that in the past I may have attached more importance than was healthy to wondering what other people might think of me just because I changed my mind. Those who are close to me know that I am an ever-changing, always growing person. Changing my mind is one part of my own decision-making process that involves boundaries, integrity and flexibility.

The Affirmation — I don't want what I don't want.

The Reflection — In making choices you may really believe that you *really* want some element of the situation. But in actuality it is most convenient for you to *believe* you want it. Take a friendship that has become like a pair of old comfortable shoes. Do you honestly like the shoes? Or are you just used to them? Removing layers of habits or patterns of believing may show you that you don't really want what you have been assuming you want.

The Meditation — I recognize the freedom and the responsibility that go hand in hand with making choices. I gently move past habits and assumptions I may be holding about my relationships or day-to-day activities. I consider what I don't want as part of my information in making choices. And I also give myself permission to not have to want what others think is best for me.

The Affirmation — Today I am learning to get more comfortable with my own power.

The Reflection — The thought of claiming and making use of your own power may be scary. Perhaps it reminds you of an old need to be defensive or omnipotent or it still remains synonymous with control, competition and domination. But one of the most freeing aspects of claiming the real sources of power available to us is in coming to terms with one's limitations.

The Meditation — Each day as I journey closer to the light of healing I gain strength. It is not the power borne of shame, fear or blame but one that emerges from within and in relationship to a Higher Power. I'm not a victim to the past, nor subject to the whims, worries or manipulations of others. I don't have to take the world the way in which it is handed to me.

*The Affirmation — My sexual behavior
is a direct reflection of the way I feel
inside.*

The Reflection — "Mechanisex" sounds to me
like a good word for mechanical sex. I've heard
men and women at times both complain about
someone wanting them sexually only where
there was a lot of technique but no real intimacy. Perhaps it is safer than the raw vulnerability of what it means to be within one's own
skin, fully alive and vibrating with all sorts of
human experience.

The Meditation — I take time to notice how I
express my sexuality and the ways I am tempted to act mechanically. Acting mechanically is a
window to my fear of who I am or of what I
will find by daring to be intimate. I may choose
to put aside my sexual behavior for a while in
order to let the person within my body come
out of hiding so that I am the person I truly
want to be in and out of the bedroom.

> *The Affirmation — I am willing and able to speak for myself.*

The Reflection — Speaking for ourselves involves risk. It means being visible and vulnerable. Many of us have learned of the importance of using "I" statements as we became involved in personal growth. Saying "you" when we really are referring to ourselves is a form of denial. We need to remember that we are adults living in the present. Our inner child can teach us what our needs are. But we can express ourselves from the point of power that starts with "I."

The Meditation — Today I will listen to my wants, needs, feelings and experience from my inner child and express these feelings through my adult self. I do not avoid the present moment by referring to my feelings through the child. I will not exploit myself by dumping the responsibility for myself today onto my inner child.

> *The Affirmation — I am electric, vibrating with the energy of the universe.*

The Reflection — I like to walk outside on a sunny day and marvel at how electric I feel — healthy, fully alive, free to move in my surroundings. It's easy to get caught up in the fast pace, the demands of mundane activity, taking things like this for granted. When I'm in touch with the current of life, I wonder how I can ever greet the day without appreciating how infinitely wise and creative the universe is.

The Meditation — The very fact that I continue to breathe is an indication that I am "plugged in," electrically vibrating with the current of life. I am a part of the universe. From the top of my head to the tips of my toes, from sunrise to sunset, I am connected with life. My expression and perceptions are important statements I make about what I believe my place within the universal life-force to be.

The Affirmation — I let the communication that goes on beyond words stretch me beyond the mundane.

The Reflection — Many times when I communicate with my guide dog, lyndi, I'm amazed at how powerful the communication between us can be, even though it is beyond the most commonly recognized day-to-day verbal communication as we know it. It often reminds me of the very subtle ways messages are transmitted between people and the other dimensions of awareness — intuition, instincts, psychic perception.

The Meditation — I listen to the substance beyond the verbal that reaches out for my attention. I learn to take those subtle perceptions and instincts that just tickle around my ears for my recognition. I am learning to stretch my awareness as I continue to enrich my communication.

*The Affirmation — There is always more
of life than what I am presently aware of
in this moment.*

The Reflection — I'm suggesting that we keep
an expansive view, an open window to what
may lie just beyond the present moment waiting
to be recognized. I decided to get my guide
dog after an intuitive flash, something I had not
even considered five minutes before it occurred. I just recently hooked up my modem
and began to find information and new friendships. It leads me to wonder what other surprises I will find beyond what I assume the big
picture to be.

The Meditation — I slow my pace down and
take heart that there are always more surprises
in store for me than I can even imagine. They
come when I am ready to receive them and
show me I can always learn more than I have
assumed. I keep an open mind and an open
window to the fresh air surprises that may blow
into my life.

> *The Affirmation — I let my limitations come out from the background and work for me.*

The Reflection — Though I have lived with blindness since childhood, I have not adjusted to it automatically as some people have wanted to assume. I have grappled to grow in self-acceptance and frequently found that all people have their own particular disability. We all have our scars, parts we'd just as soon get rid of or hide from others.

The Meditation — I make a conscious effort to celebrate myself today, taking into account the limitations I have wanted to hide or bury. Each time I am bombarded by the fear and ignorance of others who don't know what to do with my limitations, I take it as an invitation to love myself more. I honor the viable place differences and limitations have in the universe.

> *The Affirmation — I keep my spirits high and myself enthusiastic, knowing that positive outcomes are always possible beyond my immediate projections.*

The Reflection — How many times have I been so sure that the things I most dreaded would be the actual outcome, only to find I was obsessively scaring myself once again. No matter what balanced perspective someone would offer, I was so sure what I saw was the only possible outcome. Today I successfully interrupt the pattern from a vantage point of faith, to find later that I have saved myself so much energy.

The Meditation — I am kinder to my body, to my spirit and to my relationships when I save myself needless abuse when lapsing into old patterns of projection. I am calm and open to the present moment, trusting that I am being divinely protected and led to my highest good.

The Affirmation — I take time to feel my spirit, to stay in touch with who I really am.

The Reflection — Perhaps the metaphor of putting our feet into the sandy beach can be carried over into what it means to stay in touch with ourselves. When I feel the sand between my toes, I know I am truly alive. I am experiencing myself in a way that is not bogged down with shoulds, analytical pursuits or mundane responsibilities. The sand between my toes means I'm not outside my experience; I am in touch with it, in contact.

The Meditation — I put my feet into the sand today by taking time to consider who I really am. All the outward pursuits and activities can wait. They will be there when I choose to turn my attention to them. I allow myself time to drink from the well of nourishment by connecting with who I really am.

The Affirmation — I respect my own needs for personal safety and set boundaries to achieve it.

The Reflection — So many of us have lived with confusion, chaos, personal violation, encroachment on our sense of selfhood and the feeling of being emotionally threatened. Working towards a sense of personal safety in our lives has not been easy, especially in close, intimate relationships. Expressing safety needs does so much healing for us.

The Meditation — I'm often so tempted to get involved in the seeming demands of the moment. What other people are saying, what they seem to be needing may tempt me to ignore my own needs for safety. Thus I may be in the habit of sitting on much of my own experience. As I pay more attention to my needs for personal safety, I have more of it to give in relationships and more respect for my own boundaries.

The Affirmation— Feeling stupid is only a window to my fear and my anxiety about being "found out."

The Reflection — It's very comfortable to be on the "knowing" end of things, where you can show someone else what you know. But what about when you're on the "ignorant" end and you have to show what you don't know in the face of others' knowing? Remember how in adolescence we compared ourselves with others as a way of determining our okayness? Here's a window to the fear of not being good enough.

The Meditation — I remember to be gentle with myself about what I don't know. I can use my fear to monitor my need for self-validation. I remind myself of the excitement of learning when I feel myself starting to make comparative judgments of my own capabilities. I choose to accept and validate my fears as a vehicle to remain open to the process of discovery.

The Affirmation — I am safe to say no.

The Reflection — Assertive behavior is situational. Sometimes I find someone will ask me a
question and I will give them what they want
against my better judgment. This is self-violation. In that scary moment I feel I must have a
valid reason in order to spare any possible
negative consequences of saying no. What's
important is to find a sense of balance. Always
being assertive is no more or less healthy than
always being passive.

The Meditation — I know that today I'm the
best person to determine what I need and
want. I don't have to let others decide things for
me that go against my better judgment. I can
take the risk of saying no. I can take the necessary time to collect my thoughts and feelings
before answering. I respect the requests of
others and my own rights to integrity, privacy
and safety.

The Affirmation — I create positive habits in order to improve my health and move towards wholeness.

The Reflection — It is so tempting to make new changes out of fear. With all sorts of diseases and threats of what will happen if we don't eat right or take care of ourselves well enough, it is no wonder some of us have taken drastic steps. We need to weigh the effects these changes will have on our daily lives, our relationships and work habits as well as our own sanity. Making a change motivated by wanting to avoid sickness rather than moving towards wholeness only creates more stress in our lives.

The Meditation — I put aside the temptation to change my habits out of fear. Running on fear tends to make me rigid and obsessive. I listen to my body and my moods in response to what I do. I make choices that involve care-filled, thoughtful planning.

The Affirmation — *I mean what I say and am learning better ways to say what I mean.*

The Reflection — Soon after angry words are spoken, someone will frequently say, "I didn't mean what I said; I'm sorry." I maintain that at some level we did mean what was said, but we just didn't know how to manage our feelings, words and decisions so as not to be hurtful and still have a sense of peace.

The Meditation — As I take time to honestly know what my feelings are, it will be less likely that I am caught in an embarrassing moment where my expression is out of control. While it may be tempting to be totally rational, I know I have many different feelings, thoughts and reactions. Freudian slips, outbursts of emotion — these are signals that it's time to pay attention to what I really mean and to respect the many aspects of my experience.

> *The Affirmation* — *I feel thankful to-wards all the people who have contrib-uted and continue to contribute in my life.*

The Reflection — We like to hear that we're appreciated. Yet most of us also know what it's like to have someone tell us, "You should be grateful." It's often said as though you were inherently unworthy and so should be grateful. But being grateful implies joy, renewal, inner peace and celebration. It is about clearing out the clutter of resentment and triviality and let-ting in the fresh, lighter air. It sets the tone for more good to enter into our lives.

The Meditation — I express my joy and thank-fulness for all that my friends offer on a regular basis. I don't wait until they're dead to wish I had shared my gratitude. I give gifts, compli-ments, and joy just for the spontaneous pleas-ure of doing so.

The Affirmation — I respect my words as symbolic pictures of my experience.

The Reflection — Once when feeling rejected by someone, I said to a friend, "I can't believe it, the guy only put half an arm around me." What I intended to say was, "He only put one arm around me," or "I only got half a hug." Instead it came out as "half an arm." Perhaps that's how it felt. Today it's a favorite line between my friend and I, always followed by lots of laughter.

The Meditation — I notice my words. I may be tempted to shrug them off when I trip over my tongue and say things I don't mean. But later, in privacy, I can come back to them and use them as windows to my experience. While they may not be literal reflections, perhaps they will provide pictures which help me reframe my own experiences.

The Affirmation — I rely on the team-work of my own internal resources.

The Reflection — Sybil was so ingenious. It's as though parts of her took turns filling in, substituting others when the level of pain in her life became intolerable. Imagine how necessary creative defenses and the ability to disassociate from ourselves can be in order to keep going. Now, with a greater sense of consciousness, we can stay awake to our experience and allow those various aspects of ourselves to work together as a team.

The Meditation — I consciously put all of the good team building skills to work for myself. Listening, allowing for various points of view, cooperation, respect — these all are inherent in the way a good team is successful. I know I have different parts of me that all contribute to where I am in life and what I am doing with my life today.

The Affirmation — *I realistically look at what needs to get done and set reasonable priorities on my "lists."*

The Reflection — It's so easy to make that long list of all you want to get done. Suddenly you find yourself in the middle of lots of pieces you want to see completed and don't know which way to turn. Then comes the disappointment, the self-talk about being incompetent or maybe just a sense of discouragement.

The Meditation — I quiet the race in my mind and look at my desires and expectations. What am I hoping to accomplish today? Will I need help from anyone else? If the answer is no to any of these, I look at what needs to get completed most quickly. What has been on hold a long time already that needs to move higher on my list? I make my decisions about this day and put those other items on hold.

> *The Affirmation — I look at the direction of any given relationship before I decide to say everything I can think of as a retort or response.*

The Reflection — Once when perplexed about how a teacher had graded me, I discussed with my therapist all the things I felt like saying to this teacher. My therapist asked me if I wanted this person to be a friend of mine or only a teacher. I was clear I didn't want to spend social time with this teacher. We then discussed how to handle my response more professionally and less defensively than if I had wanted a friendship.

The Meditation — I closely look at what I want out of various relationships. Even when I may not like people's values, opinions and assumptions, I am less frivolous with my emotional energy. I realize I have wasted enough of it in the past with the need to be defensive and self-protective.

> *The Affirmation* — *The activity of living is always taking place in my life and within the universe.*

The Reflection — There is something about the continual music of my large wind chimes that affirms the constant activity of life. Whenever I may doubt there is any forward movement toward positive change, those musical sounds tell me change is always taking place.

The Meditation — If I am discouraged about how slowly things seem to be working towards positive change, I notice the testimony to life that continues within and around me — the sun that rises and sets automatically, the resilience of the human body, and how much of its own functioning goes on without any help or control from me. How many times have I just happened to be in the right place at the time where I could receive what I needed to take that next step? The activity of life is always happening.

> *The Affirmation — I let positive relation-ships help me heal any broken pieces of my past.*

The Reflection — If you've ever told someone a secret and felt relieved to have your words and feelings met with understanding, then you know the healing that comes from sharing your inner self in positive relationships. The forgive-ness, the knowledge that you're not alone, the awareness that your life does make sense — all these do so much to heal the past.

The Meditation — I remember the feelings I got from the experience of emotionally sharing with someone. I am often tempted to hide my feelings and emotionally isolate myself when I feel vulnerable. But carrying secrets and need-ing automatic defenses belong to the past. To-day in my commitment to personal growth, I choose to consciously break that old cycle by letting new friends be there for and with me.

The Affirmation — I proudly wear my uniform and do the job I'm here to do.

The Reflection — One day I came to believe that blindness is my uniform. It's something I agreed to wear, to take on this life as a responsibility in order to do the work I'm here to do. It is not the bottom-line definition of who I am, but it is what I wear to do my work in life.

The Meditation — I take time out to consider my uniform. It may be a particular circumstance in life that has taught me empathy, survival, kindness, the gift of humor, what it means to think on my feet or intuition. All these are components of my resources and I accept these as part of my uniform. I wear my uniform proudly, doing my best work while in it. At the same time I realize I am much more than my uniform. It is only the vehicle I use to get my work done.

The Affirmation — My anger works for me when it helps me to take positive action.

The Reflection — So often I hear people trying to do away with their anger, measuring their personal growth in terms of how long they have been able to go without getting angry. Then when they find themselves angry, they either make a feast of their rage or shame themselves for not transcending anger the way they believe they should have.

The Meditation — I let my anger work for me by being aware of it. It lets me know how tired I am of old ways that no longer work. I need to use my anger as energy to make positive change, as the fuel to propel me forward. I can change habits, undo the influence of old messages, confront my fear as I allow my anger to empower me. Anger is only destructive for me when I hold onto it and keep it buried.

The Affirmation — I am present. I pre-sent myself.

The Reflection — We use the word present to mean many different things in a variety of sit-uations. "Here is a present." "Now I present myself to you." "I receive many presents." "I feel your presence is always with me." Within the word presence is the notion of essence. Also contained in the word presence is "sense." It's as if in order to be truly present requires staying in touch with both one's essence — that which reflects the spirit — and one's sense, common or otherwise.

The Meditation — I am present. I am awake and aware of what is going on within and around me. As I am present, I am able to be a present as I give my full attention to my rela-tionships and my work. I am centered in how I present myself because I feel the presence or essence of my Higher Self within me.

> *The Affirmation — Light is always good
> for me.*

The Reflection — Light is an interesting word.
Light, meaning not heavy and light, meaning
not dark, are both good for us. I supposedly
lost my light perception when my eyes were
removed some 18 years ago and replaced with
artificial ones. Yet many times when meditating
I see light patterns moving before me. And I
have learned to trust the blessings of light and
all that it illuminates from within myself.

The Meditation — The word light is a key
word that brings my focus back into perspective. Light is always good for me so I keep my
mood light, my thoughts light. I eat light and
give the light touch to my own expectations of
myself and of others. I use inner light to improve my own vision, that is my self-under-
standing. I use light to appreciate beauty in
others and in the universe.

The Affirmation — The most important part of my sexual identity is what's between my ears.

The Reflection — The definitions and expectations of what it is to be a woman or a man in today's society have changed. A number of trends have cast doubt on our concepts of masculinity and femininity. Coming to terms with one's sexual identity is not just a matter of which set of organs we inherited or the size and frequency of their use. It revolves around what goes on between our ears, not our thighs.

The Meditation — How do I feel about myself today? Am I hoping to wear the right clothes, perform in just the right way so that someone approves? It's time to clearly use my adult self to remind my child that my feelings of shame and inadequacy belong to the past. I let what's between my ears carry the meaning of the experience I bring into the bedroom and into all my relationships.

The Affirmation — Positive change happens automatically with even the slightest indication that I am willing to allow it.

The Reflection — It's amazing that as soon as you express the slightest interest or willingness, positive change moves in automatically. It's the willingness that happens in healthy relationships when compromising goes on. As long as you are stuck in believing that willingness means having to like or agree with the change immediately, there is no room for possibility. It either is or it isn't.

The Meditation — Perhaps I have put changes off because I have been hoping I would finally talk myself into liking what I cannot seem to accept. I look back on other changes I have made, noticing some that have taken much hard work and others that have happened automatically. I remind myself it doesn't all have to be hard work — a little willingness can go a long way.

> *The Affirmation — I am open to finding inner guidance through a receptive emotional posture.*

The Reflection — So often have I tried to "get centered." I have prayed furiously, asking for something positive. I've gritted my teeth and declared affirmations. When I feel centered, I am reminded that it is a posture I find within myself and not a handout from any other source. It is the state of mind and heart out of which inner sight develops, a point by which I am able to set my emotional compass.

The Meditation — Am I trying to be receptive to my inner guidance or do I feel connected effortlessly? I remind myself that the only thing in the way between me and that connection is my own fear or self-doubt. The posture I need to feel centered comes from within me. It is a willingness to step out on the edge of life with courage.

The Affirmation — It's time for me to know what I know.

The Reflection — Affirmations are useful tools for self-empowerment. But they are only a step toward believing that I know what I know. It isn't enough for me to recite canned jargon and phrases in hopes it will become part of me. That kind of pushing doesn't come from or lead to self-acceptance. Nor will it necessarily enhance the relationships within my life without other components of self-knowledge.

The Meditation — I know what I know. I stop the chatter and commotion of words and ideas in my mind and look at what wisdom I have acquired through my experience. What has my intuition taught me over the years that can now be appreciated and integrated as knowledge? Affirmations are only one tool I can gently use with myself. They are only the training wheels needed for me to learn about balance and to develop inner strength and wisdom.

> *The Affirmation — I feel whole and alive
> when experiencing my grief.*

The Reflection — I often hear grief talked about
as though it is synonymous with pain. If it is,
then no wonder people would just as soon
avoid experiencing it. To benefit fully from the
grief process, we must let ourselves "be with"
our experience. There is pain we will no doubt
have to let go of. But there are also moments of
peace that arise out of coming to terms with
what it means to be at the very center of one's
own life.

The Meditation — I trust myself to experience
and express grief as a part of my life. I can let
the love of others be there for me in times of
grief. My grief gives me a doorway to all that is
inside of me. The vulnerability I feel is the
ticket I need to grow and expand.

> *The Affirmation — I desire to see, grow, know and live.*

The Reflection — When we truly love and desire something, it grows and manifests in unlimited possibilities. It has been said metaphysically that desire is "Of the Father" or "Inner promptings of the Spirit." In this sense, desire is borne of inspiration, without the goal of possession or covetousness in mind. Desire does not mean we sit idly waiting for good fortune. True desire requires commitment, dedication and the discipline to work with inspiration towards unlimited possibilities.

The Meditation — I let my desire work for me. Rather than feeling ashamed for what I want, I validate my desires, knowing they truly make sense to me and reflect my survival and the meaning of my life. I know that the more honest joy I feel about what I desire, the more it will grow.

The Affirmation — I stop "shoulding" on myself and decide those things that are best for me.

The Reflection — The first time I heard some-one say, "Stop shoulding on yourself," I had to laugh. Ragina Ryan writing about a terrible pain in her shoulder, in the publication *The Wellness Workbook,* discovered this. She noticed that "The bulk of the word shoulder is should." Now, when I notice that familiar discomfort in my shoulders from too much responsibility, I remind myself to stop "shoulding."

The Meditation — How much of the world have I been carrying on my shoulders? Do I hear a voice saying: "You should do . . . , you should be . . . ?" These kind of messages mean, "Don't be . . ., Don't be who you are." Today as I embrace the task of truly taking care of myself, I put the "shoulds" out of my way and look at what is best for me.

The Affirmation — I allow myself to learn from the imperfections of leaders.

The Reflection — Leaders are human too. Oftentimes we don't want them to be human, at least not fallible. We sing their praises for a while until we don't like something they did or didn't do or said. And we may find ourselves righteously scrutinizing and judging some aspect of their lives on moral grounds. Even if we choose to place them on a pedestal, that doesn't necessarily mean they are obligated to live by *our* standards.

The Meditation — How do I view those who have influenced what I now know? Have any of them disappointed me? If one of them is unfriendly or displays behavior that is against my values, I can learn about my own boundaries and priorities from this. I can also let their humanness give me permission to be imperfect and expand my own sense of self-acceptance.

211

The Affirmation — We are all teachers and students. As I learn, so too will I teach others and honor my studentship in life.

The Reflection — It is so tempting to look at relationships and say: "Now you are the teacher and I am the student" or vice versa. Not only are teaching and learning interchangeable within any given relationship, but they often happen within the same moment. The difference between student and teacher may only be a matter of our own awareness of the essential relationship between self and the process of learning.

The Meditation — I am a teacher and a student of life. What I say and do are always teaching others, even when I am not consciously aware of it. I teach as I express all that I continue to learn about myself. At the same time, I am also a student. I learn from the direct and indirect messages I get from others and from life. I learn from mistakes and successes.

> *The Affirmation — I look beyond the
> obvious and find imagination, resources
> and survival.*

The Reflection — I see the child in most adults,
no matter how big or how old they are. Likewise, I see the adult in most children — that
man or woman making decisions, taking charge
and expressing life in all its fullness. These are
the mutually energizing paradoxes within us all
from which we can draw at any time. We only
need to keep our eyes truly open and our
hearts willing to see beyond the obvious.

The Meditation — I look beyond the obvious
in others and see potential. I gain understanding about that little child within each adult, and
that full-fledged adult within each child. Without analysis and intellect, it is easy to see from
whence they came, or where they may be
headed. As I look beyond the obvious, I am
reminded how whole and sophisticated we are.

> *The Affirmation — I choose the freedom
> side of letting go.*

The Reflection — The thought of letting go
has always been met with ambivalent feelings. I usually heard advice about letting go
when I feared I would only be engulfed,
violated or abandoned. It sounded like doing
without, giving up, surrendering to the control of others. But the letting go that takes
place in the absence of fear is what leads to
lightness and freedom.

The Meditation — I know that letting go is to
find more freedom in my life — allowing someone or something to help me, giving room for
new habits to take form, feeling lighter with
the removal of something unhealthy from my
life. As I consider letting go in future experiences, I will remember that the fearful side of
letting go belongs to the past.

> *The Affirmation — I have enough en-
> couragement to see and can now go
> forward "in courage" to claim a clear
> vision of my own future.*

The Reflection — So often we use words as
nouns that would be better off as verbs —
words that lend action, power and motion to
what we mean. In a simplistic way, encourage-
ment means to be filled with courage. To encourage is to actively lend support from a basis
of caring, concern and empathy. It implies taking at least one step beyond what a person
believes to be safe. In essence, it is going
forward in courage, not unlike the process of
having faith in ourselves.

The Meditation — As I am filled to overflowing
with the courage I need, I cannot possibly fall
back into not seeing. There is enough support,
enough courage for me to trust my intuition,
my own perception and experience.

> *The Affirmation — I give and receive care so that my sense of self can be "care-filled."*

The Reflection — We often say the word careful out of fear. "Be careful," "Drive carefully," — as though trying to avoid doom or catastrophe. Why not think of being careful as meaning care-filled? Being care-filled can mean being filled with the care we give to ourselves, the care we receive from others, and the care we give to significant others and the larger community.

The Meditation — I am learning a new meaning of the phrase "Be careful." As I continue on my journey of personal growth, it is nice to be filled and surrounded with care. All of the self-care I now give myself is accumulating in my bank of health. All the care from others is also filling me up with new resources. To be "care-full" means I have enough nourishment and strength to give care to all that I do and experience.

*The Affirmation — I put the temptation
of worry aside and express my concern
in healthy ways.*

The Reflection — I believe worry adds to our
feelings of doubt, fear and mistrust. It is a false
emotion that feigns concern while hiding behind inaction. True concern, on the other hand,
means I have a perspective that may be valid. It
is motivated by compassion, empathy and the
discretion of knowing when and how to express
oneself in a loving, encouraging way.

The Meditation — I put aside the temptation to
worry. I recognize it by obsessive thought, depression or the various ways it feels and acts
out in my body. I recognize the worry of others
if I feel like defending or withdrawing from my
relationship with them. When I need to express
concern, I speak honestly from my own point
of view, allowing others to make choices and
move freely.

> *The Affirmation — I use stress to mean positive emphasis.*

The Reflection — We usually think of stress as being a negative consequence we must continually try to avoid or at best manage. But rather than looking at what stress is doing to us, we can look at it in terms of what we want to emphasize in our lives. Like a number of other so-called negative feelings, stress can be very much like a good friend who challenges us to live fully.

The Meditation — I take charge of what I want to stress in my life. I have felt passive about this decision for too long, as though life has continued to weigh me down. I can choose to place stress on the qualities I want to emulate, on the self-image I want to maintain. I can now place positive emphasis on those things that will enhance my life and how I feel about myself.

The Affirmation — I am free to love others without getting myself in the way.

The Reflection — We need enough ego to have healthy self-love, and we can never have too much self-love. It is when we have too much false ego and not enough self-love that we cannot freely love others. Self-infatuation is not the same as self-love. The former is borne of egocentric thinking and arrogant attitudes. Self-love, on the other hand, is founded in self-respect, healthy self-esteem and does not diminish others.

The Meditation — If I experience selfless love, it is a by-product of my emotional and spiritual growth. I didn't lose myself as I have when I have taken care of others at my expense. Selfless love is freeing. It is transformative, taking me beyond the confining obstacles that kept me from feeling whole and free.

The Affirmation — I wish others "good success."

The Reflection — To wish someone good luck hints that they need chance to make wishes come true, that they do not have the skills to do it. To wish means to want something to happen. It doesn't mean to whine and beg for something like a victim. Creating and generating the energy to empower your wishes and wants helps set the universe in motion. This energy is also reflected back to the individual, making you receptive to opportunities.

The Meditation — I wish others success. When anyone wishes me good luck or says that I was lucky, I remind myself that I have not just been lucky; I have been successful. This puts the onus of responsibility for the efforts and results back on me.

*The Affirmation — I enjoy the freedom
of forgiveness when I experience it.*

The Reflection — How much forgiveness is
necessary in our lives? It's a question many
people are struggling with — "Must we?" "Do
we have to?" Some contend it is necessary, and
others say it is not. True forgiveness evolves
from the heart and cannot be mandated. It
either happens or it doesn't. As true self-forgiveness sprouts from deep roots within, forgiveness towards others flowers.

The Meditation — I am open to the gifts I
receive when true forgiveness is part of my life.
I do not try to force it. My main job with
forgiveness is to forgive myself. If or when I
feel forgiving toward someone else, it is my
blessing too. I notice how much more energy I
have to enjoy the present moment with full
awareness when forgiveness takes place.

> *The Affirmation — I speak from my heart and trust my heart to speak for me.*

The Reflection — Sometimes, in our personal growth work, we can get caught up in trying to remember the past. We struggle hard to say what we want to say with all the right jargon. It can get cumbersome. When all we want is to keep it simple and merely say how we feel, the heart is the source to trust. From there we can speak clearly. The language of the heart does not have to be disguised in the dialect of useless jargon or hidden beneath worn-out buzz words.

The Meditation — I drop all the jargon and buzz words so that I can begin to speak from my heart. How do I feel in my heart about the people around me? It is so tempting to get caught up in the tunnel vision of the terms and new insights I am learning. But now I take time to simply know and express how I feel beyond all that.

> *The Affirmation — I allow myself to un-*
> *fold naturally like the bud that is a pre-*
> *lude to the blossoming flower.*

The Reflection — Are you in a rush to get somewhere with all of this emphasis on personal growth? Workshops, books, tapes, all give the message that "Life is beginning now if you embark on this." Do you discount all of the work and success you've accomplished to date? Do you feel you have to be perfect today or can you wait until tomorrow? You can slow down and stop chastising yourself for not being "well" yet.

The Meditation — I do not have to hurry. I am naturally unfolding like a blossoming flower. My insights and the resulting changes may seem slow at times, but they happen gradually and completely from a foundation deep within me. Over time, I have accumulated skills, resources, insight and awareness, to be drawn upon in the daily process of my unfolding.

The Affirmation — My money is a mirror of the abundance I believe I'm meant to have. I respect it, enjoy it and act responsibly with it.

The Reflection — What did you learn about handling money? What do you remember about those who handled money when you were small? Was money wasted? Was it used as a way to gain power or to withhold love? Did people fear the absence of money and speak in terms of the possibility of doom? Chances are that these have influenced the way you handle money in your life today.

The Meditation — I notice how I handle my money today and take steps to handle it responsibly. I enjoy my money, allowing myself to live without fear of loss. As I am willing to take charge of my money, I find it is yet another reflection of my total journey through recovery.

The Affirmation — I expect wellness in all aspects of my life.

The Reflection — I called a bookstore once to ask for a particular book on wellness. The man said he didn't understand what I was saying. I said, "Wellness, you know, the opposite of illness!" "Oh illness!" the man exclaimed, "Now I understand." His frame of reference for wellness was only grounded in the awareness of illness. Wellness is something more than the opposite of being sick. It is a conscious choice to strive towards our highest good and live in full awareness.

The Meditation — Today as I focus on improving the quality of my life, I remind myself that I am well enough to make my life better. I may have heard that I was ill. The illness label may have helped me get on the right track, but today I can affirm my health and wellness.

The Affirmation — I let the apparent obstacles of life teach me about living beyond the obvious.

The Reflection — Blindness reminds me personally that vision is in the mind. Someone who uses a wheelchair reminds me that the most important movement is in our thoughts and in our hearts. Someone who is hearing impaired reminds me that it is the inner voice to which we must listen vigilantly. George Bernard Shaw once wrote, "Defend your limitations and they will indeed be yours."

The Meditation — Today I consider what I can see beyond the obvious circumstances of my life. There may be areas where I have assumed limitations that may in fact be doorways. Having grown up in a dysfunctional family has shown me that the real home I need is within me. Abuse can teach me that the real care I receive is best chosen through my awareness.

> *The Affirmation — I am ready to fill this new page of my life.*

The Reflection — We use scrap paper all the time, making our marks, our mistakes, building our successes as we throw the scraps away. Then we fill that new page with all that we've learned. I believe we also have "scrap people" in our lives. We make our marks, our mistakes. We learn our lessons and put them aside when we're ready to move on to richer and fuller relationships.

The Meditation — I am ready to fill this new page that is before me. What I do and how I express myself will reflect what I have learned. Today's page may contain some of the people who have been there for a long time and others who have recently been added to my life as well. I may leave out some people who were there before. Whatever the case, it is my page to fill in the best way I know how.

The Affirmation — I celebrate the little moments.

The Reflection — Once in a while, when I'm hell bent on some big goal I have, there is a little moment that slows me down. It gives me spiritual nourishment beyond any big success I may have previously imagined. A moment with my dog, a walk with a friend, an insight, some time with a child — where I am suddenly expanded in my awareness. I come away feeling different, enriched, fed.

The Meditation — I celebrate the little moments. I consider some of them I've already known. I remember my vulnerability and humility as I was transformed by these experiences. I respect the power these moments hold, their ability to change my awareness and perception of people, places and things. I will also remember to appreciate my own participation in creating the little moments.

The Affirmation — I deserve to be heard.

The Reflection — "Children are to be seen and not heard." Was that a familiar line in your house? "It's grown-up hour." "You're a child. Children are not entitled to an opinion." These are phrases I heard growing up. How about you? Do you still hear them in your head today when you dare to express yourself?

The Meditation — Today I notice the indicators that tell me whether I deserve to be heard and how I feel about my right to express myself. I may be carrying a leftover belief from childhood that I do not deserve to be heard. I am no longer a helpless child. I am older now, wiser and more independent. Today there are people who want to hear me. I can let them know I need their help, that it is not always easy to express myself.

> *The Affirmation — I move through my anger to find the sources of my hurt and fear when I need to do so.*

The Reflection — Recently, my angry feelings about being short-changed led me to hurt feelings about being left out. Upon closer examination, I uncovered my fear of abandonment. Anger can be an important signal that it's time to make a change. Yet my anger may also serve as a mask, distracting me from the true sources of hurt and fear in my life.

The Meditation — I have the courage I need to go through all of my feelings and face my fear. Anger allows me to be active. I can be noisy, verbal with my expression. When I contact my hurt, I can still express it through a display of sadness. When I reach my fear I am passive in my expression. When I come through my fear with new awareness and the ability to honestly share my experience, I am more whole.

The Affirmation — I do some of my deepest, most potent growing in the soft moments of my life.

The Reflection — During a rocky interlude with a friend, we had a conversation that was a lot like many others we had shared. I felt safe enough to set aside the discomfort that had made me try to distance my friend. I melted into the present moment of being with my friend and immediately got past my hurt to the fear and knew I was free. The worst was over. I could now choose to express my fear in a responsible way.

The Meditation — I step back from any temptation to hit recovery hard and take the healing that comes in soft moments. As I hear old punitive voices in my head, it is tempting to believe I should be hard on myself. In the soft moments, I am safe enough to receive love and spiritual nourishment. I am quiet so I can hear my own experience as it is, not as I believe it should be.

> *The Affirmation* — *In my vulnerability I find unrecognized dimensions of strength.*

The Reflection — How odd it can be to experience two seemingly contradictory feelings simultaneously. I have often felt like this when it came to letting myself be vulnerable. Aware of my vulnerability — the fear of being abandoned, of not being adequate, of not coming through on goals — I have been amazed to find a sense of oneness and personal strength at the heart of it all.

The Meditation — I look in my own backyard for my hidden treasures. I realize now that instead of being a secretive, shameful part of my life, my vulnerability is a doorway to as yet unrealized strength. I have compartmentalized my experience: my childhood memories, mistakes I've made, violations I have felt, etc. But as I integrate all of these into my present understanding, skills and sensitivities, I can only grow richer.

The Affirmation — When I am talking about me, I say "I," and when I say "you," I mean you.

The Reflection — It is so easy to hide behind other people or to disguise a statement about oneself by using a generalized "you." Part of growing means daring to go out on that limb and saying what honestly belongs to me. It means getting through that gripping sense of stage fright as I dare to own beliefs, feelings and perceptions that may not be shared by anyone else at the time.

The Meditation — When I speak from an "I" standpoint, I can claim my own personal power. I also give others around me the freedom and the responsibility to own what is true for them. When I hide my experiences in generalized references, I encourage others to define their experience on my terms. Making "I" statements when that's what I really mean is an essential step towards self-empowerment.

> *The Affirmation — I practice faithfulness*
> *actively, wisely and with responsible*
> *discretion.*

The Reflection — As a child I needed to practice faithfulness toward people in irrational
ways. Those who hurt or abused me needed
to be seen as worthy of my love and loyalty. I
was not free to walk away and take care of my
own needs elsewhere. Sometimes, merely to
survive, I had to be faithful to people who did
not deserve it.

The Meditation — As an adult, I am the one
who needs and deserves my faithfulness. Spending faithfulness on others at the expense of my
own spirit and integrity is like feeding others
on my budget and allowing myself to starve.
Faithfulness requires me to actively participate
in the process of supporting myself rather than
sitting in fantasy as a spectator.

The Affirmation — I enjoy the blessings that come in the gift of simple love.

The Reflection — My guide-dog Lyndi is amazing in her ability to accept simple love. She gets her body in the positions in which she wants to receive love, rolling over to have her belly rubbed, putting her head back to have her ears scratched. She doesn't hesitate or rehearse her desires. She doesn't apologize for how much she wants or do anything right away to take care of me so that she earns her keep. She simply enjoys the love she receives with her total self in the moment.

The Meditation — Today I notice those who reach out to give me love — compliments, invitations, physical affection, even trusting my skill and judgment in something that is work-oriented. I stop the fast pace in my mind and take time to notice and receive this recognition.

The Affirmation — I am part of the ocean of life.

The Reflection — Walking beside the ocean, I am often amazed by it in so many ways. Its constant rhythm reminds me of big arms that can cradle me and rock the entire universe. As a child, when I still had light perception, I remember how the sun would shine on the water — how marvelously bright it was and how all-encompassing the reflections appeared. When I hear the sound of the waves, I consider the constancy of life. The ocean, a liquid theater of life, yet somehow it can take us beyond the pettiness of day-to-day drama.

The Meditation — I live within the ocean of life. Sometimes the waves reflect in my moods, sometimes as soft backgrounds to my peace. The ocean remains present through the dramas of my life, yet lifting me above mediocrity. I take a moment to consider how much like nature I am.

The Affirmation — *I remind myself that waiting is also a choice, an attitude reflecting my expectations.*

The Reflection — I must confess — I have always despised waiting. But that hasn't prevented many lessons from being given to me where I have had no choice but to wait. When I was born, I arrived three months early, only to find I had to stay in neonatal isolation. Today I take time to consider that waiting doesn't mean doing without or that it will take forever. Waiting is a posture of being still, an expectation-filled frame of mind.

The Meditation — I slow down my fast pace and think of the things I wish would've happened yesterday. I look at what waiting means. Today I am not at the mercy of those who could not come through for me. I can remind myself that there are options, choices I can make if the wait isn't worth the while.

*The Affirmation — I respect my uncon-
scious, knowing it holds the treasures of
my memories and resources I can use
when I'm ready to receive them.*

The Reflection — While describing the unconscious to a group of my students, I asked them
to imagine a large house with several rooms,
some of which were not regularly in use. It
made sense to close off rooms so as not to
waste heating or air-conditioning until there was
a reason for using those rooms. Keeping them
closed was a wise and protective decision.

The Meditation — I respect my unconscious.
It keeps me safe and whole, protecting me
from wasting my resources, perhaps keeping
me from being violated by others. My memories and emotional experiences are revealed
to me as I feel safe and whole enough to
unravel what is true for me in such unraveling.
I find each time how deeply and definitely I
always make sense.

The Affirmation — I stay awake to the love my total body needs and deserves.

The Reflection — How do you get the "groundedness" in the way you need to be loved? Hugs are superficial gestures where faces or heads touch while distance remains from the neck down. Sexual touching has the structure of a beginning and an end, yet often goes on without the emotional presence you need and deserve. Massage often gets lumped in with other methods of bodywork. What your body needs most is to be loved.

The Meditation — I take time to breathe and really pay attention to my body. My body holds me up day after day and deserves to be loved. Do I get the eye contact I want, the touch? I assert myself in daring to look at people with whom I want to communicate. I initiate the deeper and richer contact, being clear with myself and others as to when I feel sexual, affectionate or the need to be left alone.

The Affirmation — I look at what I get out of repeating the same painful situations.

The Reflection — When I bump my head against the same wall and continue to hope it will be different next time, I must ask myself, "What's in it for me?" Surely there is something that is keeping me from moving away from the pain and more clearly forward toward the joy.

The Meditation — I take time to reflect on any patterns where I experience the same frustrations over and over again. I look deeply and notice what's in it for me. Am I safer in it? I look at the toll I continue to pay by allowing myself to be violated by disappointing circumstances. Now is the time in my own journey to recognize the many resources, personal and professional, outside and within my own being, that I can draw upon to use this continued frustration as a platform for positive change and growth.

> *The Affirmation — I use any temptation to put others on a pedestal as a signal that it's time to work on my own self-worth and build my self-esteem.*

The Reflection — The conversation goes that you shouldn't put people on a pedestal because they usually fall off and then you're disappointed. The problem is not what we do with other people, but what we do to ourselves in this process. Putting ourselves down and assuming that others have so much power is one way we dishonor our self-worth, lower our self-esteem and show disrespect for our own integrity.

The Meditation — Who are the people I admire? Do I assume they are not ordinary? Today I remember that when I ascribe too much power to others, I fail to see how much alike we are. Just as the negatives I emphasize in others are most likely connected with me in some way, so are the positives.

The Affirmation — I stop thinking that anyone is too much or too "together" for me and see myself for the capable and powerful person that I am.

The Reflection — I can't count how many times I have thought some people were too much, too together for me. I've feared that their shoes were much too big for me. Often though, as we've gotten closer and I grew to know them well, I found that not only were their shoes not too big, they were actually too small.

The Meditation — I take my attention away from others and focus on myself. I use my perceptions of others as images to show me about how I see myself. Do I feel intimidated around others regularly? Perhaps I believe I don't know enough, wouldn't be enough in their presence. The opposite may be more true. They may turn out to be more nervous than I am about relating honestly and openly.

The Affirmation — I go through many experiences and find numerous doors that lead me to myself.

The Reflection — Have you ever wondered why you inevitably seem to continue discovering the same lessons even though the events, circumstances or people involved seem to change? There are no easy answers to this. But here it is again; that "different stuff" has fooled you into learning the same lessons yet again. Try thinking of these experiences as many doors, different pathways that are part of your journey.

The Meditation — I welcome the opening doors that lead me into the experience of my self. When I have the opportunity to learn an old lesson in a new way, I trust the universe to show me the gain in it for me today. New levels of awareness expand my recognition of the more subtle messages. These help me develop a plan to move in the directions I truly want to go.

The Affirmation — As I truly express myself I create more room for me.

The Reflection — Those who have lived in an eggshell environment would support the notion that it is wise to walk carefully, to move gingerly so as not to rock the boat or cause conflict in relationships. You may remember feeling you had to wait for the right mood so that it was okay to express yourself. But what about those moments where you've pulled out all the stops and said everything you wanted to say? You might have been afraid at first, but probably felt a great sense of relief. This often frees you to move forward in the present.

The Meditation — I create more room for myself by being myself. While eggshells may have been a main part of my survival yesterday, I know today that in my full, honest expression, I create and find my own room.

> *The Affirmation — I respect sexuality
> without fear.*

The Reflection — The belief that sex was dirty
or that people deserve to be punished for sexual behaviors, thoughts and/or feelings may
have emerged from the intuitive recognition
that we need to be constructive with our sexual
energies — not wasteful or frivolous. Often
messages that induce guilt or fear are used to
control people, to "protect" them from "harm-
ful" consequences. But to not be destructive or
wasteful with sexual energy implies a need for
respect, not guilt or fear.

The Meditation — I respect my sexuality. While
I may have felt shame or fear yesterday, today I
know it is a divine gift that puts me more in
touch with my body and takes me into experiences beyond my body. What I need is a growing appreciation, respect and reverence for the
power and meaning sexuality holds.

The Affirmation — I love my friends as flowers, appreciating them in the present and without smothering.

The Reflection — Flowers are absolutely amazing creations. Sometimes I just don't know what to do with my sense of their beauty. I can't hug them. I can smell them, remain involved almost intimately with them for the moment. Their fragrances can occasionally lift me up into new levels of consciousness and awareness. But one cannot overwhelm them, smother them or hold on to them for forever. To truly enjoy them we must be somewhat detached.

The Meditation — I love my friends as flowers. Sometimes I must simply enjoy them without interfering with their fragile lives. I can enjoy them fully in the present moment but really must let them live without any attempt to contain them. They will move through my life as through swinging doors, adding to my moments like precious flowers.

The Affirmation — I consciously take time to thank others who do things for me.

The Reflection — Since I am the only full-time person who works for me, it becomes frustrating when the help I receive from others often seems like merely part-time help. My expectations are high and my goals are many. It can then be so easy to develop resentments and a "No, thank you . . . I'd just as soon do it myself," sort of negative, ungrateful attitude. And this only makes it harder sometimes to say the appropriate and deserving "thank you" for the help I do value.

The Meditation — I need a variety of resources to achieve my goals. In my efforts to find them, I can balance any frustration by being thankful for all the help I actually receive. Part-time people helping makes for a supportive community filled with a multitude of energy and creative ideas. And for all this and more, I extend heartfelt gratitude from within.

The Affirmation — I let my love of another person heal me on the inside.

The Reflection — Have you ever noticed how loving someone helps you heal inside? It's like a cat when it knows it's safe — the claws relax, the fur goes down, the animal has no reflexive need to scare others away. I find that painful memories soften, defenses melt or mellow. And I am lighter and free to see and really care for that other person in ways that stretch me beyond my old self.

The Meditation — I think of the moments when my love toward another person has transformed me. Perhaps I am in one of those times now, or can remember what it was like. These are the moments that have truly added to me, sometimes by challenging my limits and my willingness to be intimate. I didn't need to play martyr, to sacrifice identity or desires. My attention, not merely my actions, are the point of focus here.

The Affirmation — *I let life surprise me and relish all the surprising moments of self-discovery.*

The Reflection — Have you ever noticed how often something we especially want will seemingly come into our life unexpectedly when we were least thinking about it? It's one of those ironies in life that simply cannot be ignored. For me, these are the kinds of things that will inevitably happen while I'm sleeping or in the middle of a rainstorm or some activity where I could only concentrate on what I was doing and not be obsessed with some sort of fantasy.

The Meditation — I consider the ways life has surprised me with goodies I've wanted and know that they're bound to happen many more times. The fun part is to expect that life will do its best to give me surprises when I'm most off guard. So if I relax more often and simply pay attention to what I'm doing in the present moment, any number of surprises are likely to be coming my way.

---

*The Affirmation — I find positive ways
to handle my criticism of others.*

The Reflection — How often have you stopped
yourself from expressing a critical thought or
comment because you felt that to do so would
be wrong? And the only recourse you believed
you had was to keep it inside? There are two
important things we can learn from criticism.
First, it can teach us how to recognize the
signals when it's time to make changes. Second,
it can heighten our awareness of what it feels
like to be criticized. These lessons help foster
ways of being more loving toward others.

The Meditation — I pause from the fast pace to
learn from criticism — which I have given others as well as that which I've received. I am
open to learning more positive ways to handle
things that bother me. I needn't stay silent or be
overly aggressive. I can use my tendency toward
criticism as one of many signals that it may be
time for me to make some important changes.

> *The Affirmation — The tools and equipment I need to do my job are on permanent loan inside myself.*

The Reflection — Sometimes I feel amazed at all of the resources that come up out of me at the right moments — the wisdom, the expression, the intuition. Then it dawns on me how I am given what I need to do my work. I don't have to become overwhelmed with ego or fear as I move into expanded levels of achievement. I only need merely accept that I am using what has been provided to me.

The Meditation — I am discovering the resources I have with which to do my work. My talents, sensitivity, humor, love of people — these and more are tools provided to me to use on my journey. I do not need to feel a burden of having created my abilities. There is no need for shame over what I've created or what I know. I'm trusted by a spiritual power within the universe to use these gifts wisely.

The Affirmation — I ask and listen for indications of the right use of my gifts and resources.

The Reflection — How many times have you chided yourself about opportunities or talents you thought you might have wasted? It's not that there's a limited quantity of either of these, it's only that you can never really go back to claim the joy you missed yesterday. Asking and listening for right use means learning about being your best self, respecting the planet, cultivating quality in all of your relationships and nourishing your spiritual growth.

The Meditation — I ask and listen for right use, and always receive the direction and protection I need. I am not alone and do not have to feel as though I'm tossed out in the sea of life to drift. There is purpose and direction to my life. Asking and listening for right use helps me make choices that are more in harmony with what's best for me.

The Affirmation — I make the most of moments, knowing they can never be repeated in the same way.

The Reflection — I am awed by the paradox in my beliefs: Life is eternal and yet all that truly exists does so in the here and now. Simultaneously, each and every moment can never be repeated in the same way it was originally experienced. Nostalgia is wonderful, but memories are like photographs in the mind's eye. We can reconnect with the feelings associated with the memory but we delude ourselves if we believe we can recapture the true experience.

The Meditation — I respect each and every opportunity to truly take in the present moment. As I breathe the essence of each moment into me, I notice how truly special each person is who is a part of that time. In each of those moments I have the opportunity to honor, affirm and fully celebrate the unique, paradoxical experience of being exquisitely alive.

The Affirmation — I say yes to possibility.

The Reflection — It's the little phrases that refute possibilities. "I can't believe it" when something good happens. "Fat chance *I'll* win anything!" These little phrases spoken in jest, and perhaps often stemming from our need for self-protection, are windows to limited beliefs that keep possibilities we want and can have just beyond our reach. We are entitled to claim our limitations, but the more we defend them, the more likely we will be unable to say yes to possibilities that the universe will lay on our path.

The Meditation — I choose today to stop myself from speaking or thinking in phrases in which I am tempted to sell myself short. I have desires, goals, aspirations and expectations of life and myself. When I'm afraid to let others know what these are, I can keep quiet and affirm this higher vision in my own mind.

The Affirmation — My disappointments send me clear messages that it's time to take risks and expect more out of life.

The Reflection — Disappointments tell me I haven't aimed high enough, haven't been willing to dream quite big enough or broadened my expectations far enough. The result is that I've left myself open to only receiving crumbs when I am worthy of an abundant feast. Instead of giving in to pride and the temptation to bury my head in the sand along with my dreams and vulnerability, I let my disappointments propel me on to greater risks, larger plans and clearer expectations.

The Meditation — There are plans for me that are bigger and reflect far more opportunities than any setbacks or disappointments I have known. It's important that I acknowledge and allow my *feelings* of disappointment. But the heights of experience I will reach and the destinations I will go lie *beyond* my disappointment and grief.

The Affirmation — I don't need to find something wrong *with someone else to justify my discomfort with a situation.*

The Reflection — How many times have you heard people become defensive, judgmental and critical of others when the simple truth is that the situation they're in doesn't feel right to them? Instead of saying "This doesn't feel right for me," they seem to have the need to prove their point by saying, "Look at everything that's wrong about this other person. Listen to my list." All the while, the bottom line is that they want and need to get out of the situation.

The Meditation — I do not need to find a list of what's wrong with anyone else in order to move on from a situation. My choices are my responsibility. Regardless of where the gauge is on anyone else's emotional barometer, I need to also respect our potentially different versions of what is going on. I don't need excuses, just my experience and a willingness to act on what is right for me.

The Affirmation — I do not need to decide what someone else's problem is, I only need to be honest about my own.

The Reflection — Have you ever noticed how much difficulty some people have in taking responsibility for even the smallest thing? For example, when certain people are listening to someone else, but either don't agree with what's being said or become uncomfortable with the content, they might say something like, "Wow, have you got a problem . . ." Doesn't this seem odd? The person speaking wasn't even aware he or she had a problem. Yet just because someone felt threatened, he or she decided there was now a problem.

The Meditation — Today I consider paying attention to becoming more actively receptive, neither judging, defending, accepting or rejecting the opinions, thoughts, comments or beliefs of others. I do not need to decide what someone has for a problem; I only need to notice honestly when I have one.

The Affirmation — I offer all of my positive thoughts, words, energy and actions as prayers for the highest good in everyone.

The Reflection — God does not need our prayers. It is not necessary to put in a petition for our loved ones. The very nature of the universe is to intend good for all whom we love. It can do its best work with our positive thoughts and words. Our prayers are for us. Prayer helps us to focus on a sense of purpose, gives meaning to our lives and keeps us open to messages from a higher consciousness.

The Meditation — Each time I smile, say something genuinely loving, share or create laughter, I am praying. No one needs the petition or rhetoric of my prayers. They are merely a form of communication between my internal consciousness and the larger consciousness of the universe. But the universe and the people I care about can always benefit from my positive thoughts and belief in the highest good.

> *The Affirmation — I use rituals when
> they work for me and discard them when
> they have served their usefulness.*

The Reflection — Some rituals are performed
because we are sentimental about certain
places and events. Other times, we engage in
rituals out of fear, perhaps as symbolic gestures to help control or alleviate our sense of
anxiety about something. Balance allows rituals to be used when they work for discipline,
joy and building community spirit. When used
explicitly as devices of control, they deny humanness and emotional experience.

The Meditation — I look at the patterns of my
habits, my spiritual practices or any behaviors I
frequently engage in as rituals and take stock
of what is working for me and what is no
longer useful at this time. I keep those in my
life that bring me out, move me forward and
help me step confidently into the future. I set
aside those rituals that only serve to provide
temporary security and keep me from myself.

The Affirmation — I ask clearly for what I want and need, then wait to receive what's best for me.

The Reflection — Phrases like "I wish," "If only" or others that either imply or assume you will never get what you really want because you're just a dreamer, are ways of staying stuck. You needn't be careful in asking or assume it is always out of your reach. The universe already knows, so get off the eggshells, be direct and begin to expect miracles in your life. You will be pleasantly surprised at some of the answers.

The Meditation — I stop weighing my words or being modest about what I want or need. I take time to be specific and direct in asking, knowing that I will get what I want or will receive something that is even better. I will live in full expectation of the best, anticipating and having faith that there is indeed a plan greater than what I am capable of perceiving at this moment.

The Affirmation — I let go of any petty rigid need to control or understand what garbage belongs to whom and just take responsibility for disposing of my own.

The Reflection — As I was throwing away something this morning, I found a garbage can outside, lifted the lid and tossed my stuff in it. It occurred to me that I may have put my garbage in someone else's trash can. "Should I have looked around for my own garbage can?" I wondered. Then I decided that it really didn't matter; it all goes to the same place anyway.

The Meditation — I put aside the temptation to figure it all out before getting on with what I need to do. I also pay attention to any compulsion to control, manipulate or dictate how such-and-such should happen. My life is about living, not merely organizing what's mine versus other people's issues into neat categories. I get rid of my garbage and have more room and freedom to get on with life.

> *The Affirmation — I look at my life and can see one miracle after another that has brought me to where I am today.*

The Reflection — Have you ever stopped to notice how one incredible experience just somehow led to another? You met new people who just happened to be the "right" people. Somehow through one person you found an opportunity that was just exactly what you needed. You ended up in the "right place at the right time" on many occasions and got what you needed. Miracles — one after another, they are gifts of life meant for you.

The Meditation — As I notice all the events of my life, I know that I am part of a chain of miracles. That I have found personal growth and recovery, that I continue to grow each and every day, is part of the chain of miracles. From the simplicity of my breathing to the more dramatic instances of being saved in a crisis, I look at my life and see that in every moment new miracles are taking place.

*The Affirmation — When I find myself
repeatedly wanting to talk about "them,"
I acknowledge the need to take better
care of myself and focus inward.*

The Reflection — Is there someone you know
who is always lamenting or whining about
other people? I had a friend once who did a lot
of this. I often didn't even know the people she
was talking about, so it frequently got to be a
waste of time to see her. I never could quite
figure out why she wanted to spend our energies together talking about "them." When someone continues to do this, I sometimes ask, "But
what does that have to do with you?"

The Meditation — I resist the temptation of
taking the easy way out and playing it safe by
talking about "them." Hearing myself talk about
others is a signal for me to take a more candid
look at my own truth, to look inside first. At
least then I can know that I'm doing a far better
job of taking care of myself before I go around
accusing "them" of anything.

> *The Affirmation — I pay attention to the privilege of relationships.*

The Reflection — What a gift to notice how uniquely another life goes about the business of living. I notice my working guide dog a lot and one way or the other she lets me know her various needs. And the privilege in my relationship with her comes from simply paying enough attention to respond. I feel honored to be a witness to another life besides my own. Paying attention is far more essential to the process in relationships than performance, protection or efforts to predict outcomes.

The Meditation — I remind myself to pay attention in all my relationships. I consider the privilege and richness that comes into my life through full awareness of the process in relationships. As both witness and participant, I will seek to honor those in my life by paying full attention and therefore embrace the privilege of relationships.

The Affirmation — My cravings are at rest when I am involved in fulfilling activities.

The Reflection — I have been amazed to discover how satisfied my appetites are when I'm involved in fulfilling activities. Physical labor, affection, and other important involvements that help give us a clear sense of meaning and purpose seem to reduce tendencies to "crave." While there may be more to craving than a mere channeling of activity, I've been amazed at how healthy activities help balance our needs while desires just seem to take care of themselves.

The Meditation — I consider activities that are fulfilling for me and embrace the freedom of choice these energizing resources bring into my life. My participation in such activities means there is less room for boredom, restlessness, low self-esteem and loneliness. Craving subsides as I am involved in activity that is meaningful for me.

The Affirmation — I trust the integrity and the "judgment muscles" of other people to take care of themselves.

The Reflection — Do you remember any times in your life when someone else was making decisions for you and convincing you that you were cold, hungry, tired, upset? Parents are quite good at this. No matter what you said, they were certain they knew you better than you knew yourself. Such assumptions don't encourage us to use our emotional, physical and mental muscles for making choices and dealing with consequences. Nor do they feed self-esteem or a sense of our own integrity.

The Meditation — I have my own life to lead. I put aside the temptation to live others' lives for them, knowing that other people need my acceptance and faith in their abilities, not my mistrust or attempts to control, which rob them of the sense of their own integrity. I remain mindful that the primary focus of my choice-making expertise needs to be in my own life.

The Affirmation — I receive constant direction from many sources that lead me to higher purpose, clarity and joy.

The Reflection — Change happens so rapidly in my life sometimes that it feels like one big conveyor belt forever moving me. "Fasten your seat belt," goes a message in my head. There are so many other messages along the way — just a thought here and there that tells me what to do at just the right moment. Suddenly the right help is there, the right ideas come that I was unable to fathom previously and the right people for me in that moment cross my path.

The Meditation — I expect positive outcomes. I trust and have faith that the direction I need is always available to me. I ask, remain open and listen to my intuition. I listen to those whole yet quiet thoughts that spontaneously appear in my life and provide unexpected dimensions of clarity to my ideas and to the directions I seek.

The Affirmation — *I deal honestly with the internal noise of my own fear and ignorance, finding the quiet strength that comes from my sense of remaining centered.*

The Reflection — When walking with my guide dog Lyndi the other day, I noticed a small dog barking ferociously at us. I thought about how often it is the small dogs who are the loudest and the most protective about their territory. I then considered my own responses in the face of insecurity and threat. I am a lot noisier than when I feel calm within myself.

The Meditation — I pay close attention to the signals of my own protesting — the noise, the reverberations of my discomfort — and look to the fear behind them. I acknowledge that I can feel safe in my vulnerability and that I am not small or helpless. Rather than leave myself wide open, I return to the quiet solace of being centered, drawing strength to calm the noisy beasts of my own fear and ignorance.

The Affirmation — I take turns leading and following.

The Reflection — When out walking with some friends recently, I noticed that we naturally took turns leading and following. Sometimes it felt good to walk ahead of the others, trusting they were behind me. At other times, it felt nice to hang back and let one of them show me the way. Life presents this same opportunity on many levels, although we might not be exactly sure how and when to take which role.

The Meditation — I remain open to experience leading and following in my relationships. I am part of a larger team and recognize that I have skills to be helpful as both a leader and a follower. There is much to be learned from either role. There is nourishment and joy to be found in the giving that comes with being the leader and the receiving that is part of being the follower. I strive for balance, flexibility and grace as I make each of these roles a fluid part of my relationships.

The Affirmation — My appetite is both a window to and reflection of the potential I have to work towards my highest good.

The Reflection — There's something about working in the field of addiction and psychology that makes me highly vigilant. It's as if I have to be more calculated and deliberate about certain choices — "I shouldn't be angry," "I shouldn't eat so much," "I shouldn't want so much." Getting clear on my desires and then deciding how to channel my energies to achieve them is always a learning process. But the intensity of the drive behind this is my electricity, the juice that propels the very spiritual well-spring of my own empowerment.

The Meditation — I have patience with my appetite for life, and recognize my intensity as a sign of readiness. I am open to re-channeling my desires and energies in order to maximize my potential. I can utilize the drive and desires I carry to give me vitality.

The Affirmation — Freely, and with conscious willingness, I choose to look toward the bright side of other people, myself and all situations.

The Reflection — There seem to be more than enough challenges in our daily lives. I'm struck by how they are a lot like a box of tissues — you pull one out and there's always another one sticking up right behind it. Even before I can quite regain my balance from the previous challenge life offered me, along comes another one. And there are days when the situations can remind me of that tough, nearly unchewable, gristle part of a good steak that cannot be easily swallowed or digested.

The Meditation — I find invitations to choose a bright outlook all throughout each day. I recognize that moving toward the bright side is a challenge, a project full of lessons. And I gratefully accept the freedom that is received when I allow myself to move towards the bright side of life.

*The Affirmation — I step on a path to-
wards greater freedom when I begin to
open the door on the closet where I have
stored feelings of shame, fear and inadequacy and seek understanding.*

The Reflection — The sense of being different
from other people can lead us to hide our
"differentness" in a closet and surround it with
low self-worth, fear and shame. Sadly but surely,
people whose perceptions are filtered through
fear will make a point of someone's "differentness." There is the fear that if I own it, I will be
reduced to circumstances that will restrict my
movement and growth.

The Meditation — I look behind behaviors that
are most disgusting to me, behind closets of
secret habits, fantasies or judgments of others
and find the fears that are nudging me for
recognition. I claim the freedom to be found
by stepping through the threshold and behind
my closets.

*The Affirmation — I laugh honestly,
spontaneously and joyously, reveling in
the smiles of my heart and my face.*

The Reflection — One of the things I'm known
for is my loud laugh. I think its loudness partially stems from not being able to actually see
smiles, as well as not experiencing my own
smile and its effects when it reaches others.
And I've never believed it was important to
laugh in a way that many people would consider "lady-like." Laughter gives me a feeling of
openness, keeps me connected with others,
helps create a positive atmosphere and reduces
the anxiety in tense situations.

The Meditation — I enjoy laughing in spontaneous ways. I laugh honestly when I choose
to, not worrying about whether others join me,
not forcing myself to laugh when I don't honestly find something funny. My laughter helps
me gain a lighter perspective on circumstances
that can often be taken far more seriously than
might be necessary.

> *The Affirmation — I set and keep stan-*
> *dards that are deserving of my positive*
> *worth.*

The Reflection — It's scary to set and keep stand-ards. The process demands awareness of and attention to how we feel about our own sense of self-worth. Especially in the face of others who are critical, we must be able to develop internal guides for creating our standards. Others have often told me, "You shouldn't do so much be-cause you already do more than most people." Greed or over-achievement is one thing and set-ting standards based on the goals and accomp-lishments of others is another.

The Meditation — The standards I set and live by are a mirror of my self-worth. I consciously decide to set standards to reflect my growing sense of positive self-esteem. Recognizing that I will be challenged by others to follow the crowd, I use such opportunities to strengthen my emotional muscles, communication skills and independence.

The Affirmation— It is far easier now to recognize what doesn't work in my life. And I am better equipped and better prepared to do something about it more quickly and easily than ever before.

The Reflection — There is a definition of insanity that goes something like, "I keep trying to solve the same sort of problems in the same way and with the tools that seemed to work before . . . and nothing ever changes, I keep getting the same unwanted results. Am I doing something wrong?" I have some funny memories of my ceaseless attempts at "getting something right" if I could only try hard enough.

The Meditation — It is such a relief to let my intuitive inner voice assertively direct and guide me in recognizing and letting go of what is not working for me. It is so easy to get quietly comfortable with relationships, habits, familiar expectations or any other circumstances. But I believe in the necessity and inevitability of change.

The Affirmation— I actively clarify and seek clarity for the conditions I desire and expect in my life; and I send these out into the universe.

The Reflection — There is something about being willing to charge or pay for services that communicates a baseline of self-worth. If I charge low for services or pay poorly for my possessions, it sends out a message to the universe that I am not very serious about my desires and expectations for myself. It can also be a symbolic way of looking at what I settle for in my relationships. Do I allow the same crummy things to happen over and over? Or do I trade in the negative conditions from one relationship for another, supposedly better, one?

The Meditation — I consider the messages I give the universe about the conditions I desire and expect. I notice any places where I may be giving lip service but my behavior is saying something else. It is time to upgrade my conditions to the level I deserve.

> *The Affirmation — I make a commitment*
> *to the conditions I expect and desire, then*
> *leave the doors and windows open for the*
> *endlessly possible ways they can manifest.*

The Reflection — Anticipating, believing in and setting up conditions is a necessary step in clarifying directions for our lives. Without that kind of clarity, we leave ourselves open to unwanted influences and circumstances. Yet it also makes no sense to become rigid. If we somewhat arbitrarily lock ourselves into specific ways, we actually shut the door on possibility. The result is that we can take on a kind of tunnel vision that leaves out opportunities.

The Meditation — I work to achieve clarity in and clarification of what I want and expect, remaining open to the possibility of discovery. As the pictures become more clear in my mind's eye, my outward expressions of the conditions I seek to create in my life are more precise and open-ended. I am receptive to the creative process leading to fruition.

The Affirmation — I trust the big picture to work out, expanding beyond the horizons of even my own fear or anxiety.

The Reflection — Faith is not merely trusting in life when all is going well. The trust that things will not only be okay but might turn out in ways beyond our expectations comes from deep within each of us and grows through faith in ourselves.

The Meditation — I listen honestly to my feelings, giving the necessary recognition to any doubts and fears I may be experiencing. I also take into account the many times my life has worked out in spite of how grim things seemed. I choose, wherever possible, to put my best foot forward and make the most of today. Many times I have been surprised by positive outcomes that were surely beyond my expectations or my imagination.

The Affirmation — I gain a new perspective when I reach out to someone else.

The Reflection — Did you grow up with the sort of statements that were supposed to shame you, such as, "There's always someone worse off than you" or, "Think about someone else for a change"? The irony of it was that beyond chipping away at our self-esteem, there is a lot of wisdom in them. I see no such thing as too much constructive selfishness. I can't feel comfortable being nasty or insensitive to others when adequately taking care of myself. But there is so much perspective to gain from reaching out to someone else.

The Meditation — I make a commitment to reach out today to an old friend and to get back in touch on a social basis with one or more people from relationships in which I have been lax. I let this broadened horizon work for me in expanding my current perspective as I listen with my whole self grounded in the present.

The Affirmation — *I do little things differently to experience the process of change and appreciate new dimensions of awareness that open up for me.*

The Reflection — A small change in normal routines and habits can produce amazing differences in our awareness. This can include doing something last that was always done first, eating differently or even brushing your teeth with the other hand. Little changes raise the level of self-confidence and keep the door open for the bigger, more exciting changes to come in later.

The Meditation — I allow myself to make little changes that can work for me. I imagine my capacity for change to be like a muscle that needs some regular exercise to face the bigger demands on it later. I am creative with ideas of little things I can change and grow in anticipation of the greater number of changes for which I am becoming ready.

The Affirmation — I take risks that are sometimes messy.

The Reflection — Taking risks that are messy is a confirmation of our humanness — the earthy, unrehearsed, raw and frequently less-than-glorious side of ourselves. Getting angry at someone, losing control to the point that we forget our newly-learned communication skills — these are examples of risks that can be messy. If life is to be lived, it will get messy sometimes. If it is merely to be observed and used for performance, then a polished look is what we may want. But while working on the shine, let's be on the lookout for those messy human qualities.

The Meditation — I own the mess from my risk-taking. I can take responsibility for cleaning up after myself, then practice enough self-forgiveness to enable myself to move forward. I remind myself that I walk through the hallways of the school of life as both teacher and a student. I remain mindful that my life is meant to be fully lived.

> *The Affirmation — I make new changes
> in my life as I expand my willingness and
> receptivity to incorporate them effectively.*

The Reflection — The persuasiveness of a
speaker, a book that tells you why nothing
you're doing is "really" working, peer pressure
to change — all these can give you a feeling that
you've been doing it all wrong. Anxiety builds
and you wonder if you should undo all of your
life-patterns to find your place on the band-
wagon. As I look at such anxiety with hindsight
I can appreciate the fear and also reflect on how
I have taken risks and produced needed change
in moments where I feel receptive.

The Meditation — I use the persuasiveness
around me as an invitation to become centered
in my own experience. While ideas presented
to me may be worthy of my consideration, I
recall that I have made my best changes from a
platform of my own integrity and self-worth. I
am receptive to making changes in my life that
are truly good for me.

> *The Affirmation — I appreciate the wisdom hindsight has to offer and see it in its proper perspective.*

The Reflection — There is much wisdom in hindsight. It is tempting to want to take the frustration and hard work out of moving forward by pushing the wisdom and lessons of hindsight onto self or others. Yet rarely are there shortcuts that allow forward movement where insight, awareness and integrity operate in a blended fashion.

The Meditation — It is good when I have workable chunks of wisdom from my past lessons that make sense to me with hindsight. I appreciate this wisdom in its perspective, remembering that my wisdom has come from experience. I give myself and others the freedom to continue to gain from life experience.

The Affirmation — I mother myself and embrace the strength of the nurturance I can give myself when necessary.

The Reflection — Sometimes the old unfilled spaces in my life show me much about what I can give myself today as an adult. Getting away from the noise of other people's lives and direction, taking time to appreciate the risks and hard work I have performed — these are aspects of mothering myself. Others may be able to take care of me in any given moment, but such moments deserve my choice and expression about what care works best for me. Deciding how I will spend my time, energy and my role in relationships are a few of the aspects of how I can mother myself.

The Meditation — I listen to my body, my emotions, my beliefs and my thoughts. I respect the continuity of all of the changes I've made, the crises I've survived and the wisdom I've gained. I give myself the mothering I need and deserve, allowing others to care for me as I so choose.

The Affirmation — I stop pushing myself.

The Reflection — It occurred to me recently as I was trying to push some things to happen faster that I was also pushing myself way too hard. So what will be there at the end of the rush when I've achieved my goals? Probably exhaustion and a letdown from not being able to smell the flowers along the way.

The Meditation — The degree to which I find myself frustrated by circumstances and the timetable of others as they do or do not complete tasks according to my desires is a measuring stick I can use in looking at how fair I am being to myself. If I am pushing others, frustrated with what seems to be the slowness of their achievement and accomplishment, I am pushing myself too hard. It's time to settle into the flow of things happening as they will and to enjoy smelling the flowers along the way.

The Affirmation — Temptations are invitations to help me make sure I am serious about my desires and expectations. I won't settle for less.

The Reflection — It's been interesting to notice how the same temptations tend to reappear in life — to spend time with someone who's convenient but not a person of choice, to buy something on sale but not something of priority, etc. When I say no to these temptations, I feel as though I won something. The picture of my self-worth gets brighter with each triumph because the message I give back to the universe is that I really mean what I say I desire.

The Meditation — I give clear messages to the universe about my desires and expectations so I can truly be trusted to receive and wisely use my gifts. Resisting temptations are but practice opportunities for me to clarify that I will not settle for less than the best I'm worth, what I am capable of contributing and what I deserve to enjoy.

> *The Affirmation — I resist any tendencies to be calculating and mechanical in my relationships and remain open to the fluidity of life.*

The Reflection — I was writing the other day and found myself saying something about "upgrading" self-worth. I wondered if I've been around computer technology just a bit too long. All too often I hear people making the process of human interaction sterile and mechanical, when really it is the human spirit that is touched through love once one decides to accept help or create positive change.

The Meditation — I am open to life in ways that allow me to respond in the moment. I am vulnerable, non-calculating, non-mechanical in my relationship to myself and in my interactions with others. In my willingness to accept help and create change in my life, I invite the touch of other human spirits.

The Affirmation — I can take all the time I need before answering a request or a question.

The Reflection — Do you ever feel put on the spot when someone addresses you with a request or a question? It feels not okay not to have an answer or something affirmative to offer in return. There is pressure, shame, anxiety. But do we put the same pressure on others? How often do they not come through with yes to what's been requested? How often do they not know the answers and you back off to recognize their humanness, their integrity and their right to simply not know everything.

The Meditation — I take time to pause when someone asks me a question or when my involvement is requested. Today I am an adult, not subjected to the pressure that I may have felt when I was a child. Taking time before answering anything impulsively or out of a sense of urgency allows me to make sure my decision is most right for me.

The Affirmation — My journey is circular.

The Reflection — Some people seem to believe
and talk about recovery as if it were a clear-cut,
single-dimensional, linear process and then
have the audacity to judge and shame other
people. If others haven't taken a particular step,
then they must not be "in recovery." Or if they
decide to take a certain direction to deal with
another aspect of their life, then they are "be-
ginners." We are on a circular journey. It may
spiral, it may have many layers, but it is not
linear or seen accurately with tunnel vision.

The Meditation — I give myself credit for all
the progress I've made thus far. My journey is
based on what's right for me. I do not need to
get caught up in fad or the latest recovery
fashion in choosing my steps. As I continue to
move in circular ways, I take all of the wisdom
and unanswered questions with me and am
always involved at the center of my experience.

The Affirmation — Change works best as I have time to integrate my awareness into daily living.

The Reflection — We're moving so far on many levels simultaneously with this odd sense of urgency about "getting it right." Change is taking place rapidly and we are having giant leaps in consciousness as we alter our awareness. Yet while crisis and trauma may help us to pay attention, they don't do anything positive for self-esteem or spiritual growth. As we beckon to any call that says we've been "doing it all wrong," we enter into yet another dependency where someone or something else has control over our thinking, responsibility and freedom to make choices.

The Meditation — I take time to make my changes. While I am learning about better ways to live, I can let myself go slowly, trusting that I have my entire life to "get it right." The most successful changes I've made were integrated with awareness and enhanced my self-esteem.

The Affirmation — Balance in my life frees me from addiction and the tendency to think in addictive ways.

The Reflection — There is much controversy as to what constitutes addiction. Is it a medical term? Is it a bio-chemical term? Is it a philosophical concept suggesting we are challenged with every step to balance each aspect of our lives? I suppose it is all of these and that at one level perhaps the term is irrelevant. What matters is that we become conscious of what needs to change, get whatever help we need and get on with living.

The Meditation — I use my awareness of addiction to view my life in terms of striving for balance. An area out of balance means it is time to focus on what has driven me away from the present moment into the extreme. I strive for balance in my life by being open to possibility. The balance I seek takes care of itself as I acquire the help I need to get on with living.

> *The Affirmation — I am my own best healer.*

The Reflection — Once when I burned my hands with scalding milk, I suddenly created a meditation for myself where I imagined that every time I exhaled, the pain was coming out through my fingertips. The next morning I awoke and was better and pain-free. How much more of a capacity for healing ourselves from the inside might we have? And tapping into these inner resources for relieving physical pain may only be the most basic use of our capacities for self-healing.

The Meditation — I recognize a reservoir of power within me to heal myself. This means I trust my creativity and the natural rhythm of my breathing to do wondrous works. Being open to wisdom means I can also receive help when needed, but it is a synergistic help which allows the best from my spirit within to work with my Highest Power.

The Affirmation — I maintain personal respect for the true and gradual working out of my life's challenges.

The Reflection — Personal growth is not like doing the laundry and putting it away until the next time it piles up. It is not a commodity to be expressed as a calculated outline of activity. I hear issues such as forgiveness discussed sometimes as though it is a technical procedure done in a sterile, prescribed way, never to be repeated again. I don't buy it. Life's challenges tend to get repeated. And there is insight and new life experience to reap from the many different layers of any one lesson.

The Meditation — I let go of any tendency to be hard on myself about where I am in my growth process. I may want to compare myself with others, to think that I have failed. I choose to remember that healing is gradual, allowing me to build change slowly from deep within me.

> *The Affirmation — I am free to make choices about the intimacy I want in my life, knowing that quality intimacy takes much time and energy.*

The Reflection — I sometimes wonder if there isn't so much fad in the personal growth arena of life that people really believe instant intimacy is possible or even desirable. Has human experience been so mass-produced that we believe intimacy is happening when we rattle off jargon about our "child within"? It is not a jargon-filled list of the latest analysis of self or others. Intimacy is an ability and allowance of what it means to be vulnerable with another person over time.

The Meditation — I stand back from the fast pace of people sharing, networking, gossiping or from any demand or pressure I feel that I "should" be intimate with many. I consider the moments when I have felt safe to be vulnerable and compare them with how I feel in the noise of everyday chatter.

The Affirmation — *I trust my ability to get to home base within me.*

The Reflection — I believe it is possible to "come home" without taking drastic measures. But suppose there are people and times in life when this is not possible. There are moments when I say, "You know, suicide would simplify a lot of things." Thankfully, it is only a flickering thought. But could it be that for the person who chooses it as an alternative it is a way of merely returning to home base?

The Meditation — I trust my ability to find home base within me. I remind myself that I can take quiet time. I can slow down, reach within or outside to others for support. If I am overwhelmed by the drastic measures someone took in order to get to home base, I console myself by remembering that it was perhaps the best alternative they had at the moment.

The Affirmation — *I actively take the initiative to say what I really want others to know.*

The Reflection — Sometimes I ask myself, when debating about taking a risk, what I would want to say to a particular person if I knew he or she was about to die. This is not meant to turn up the panic and anxiety that goes along with abandonment, but it often encourages me to get to the heart of what I really want them to know. Perhaps as a culture we're concretely taught the importance of not wasting time by remaining all too passive with the expression of our selves.

The Meditation — I allow the statement, "I'll be honest with you," to include the rich emotional spectrum of my experience as I reach out to others. I do not wait for people, circumstances or events to pave the way or set the tone. I actively listen to my desire to reach out in a way that is enriching and freeing to myself and to others involved.

*The Affirmation — I trust the gradual
process of time.*

The Reflection — I figured out recently that
one of the few things that can happen overnight
is realizing that most things really can't happen
overnight, especially those things that are truly
valuable and meaningful. Lasting personal
growth and success in life is a slow process. So
it is with relationships, decisions and readiness
to move forward with significant changes. It
takes time. The sense of urgency in moving
forward with changes is usually grounded in
fear, not in self-esteem and self-confidence.

The Meditation — I trust the slow process of
time in creating the changes I desire. All too
often I have felt I needed to make up for the
life I believe I missed out on yesterday. In my
rush to do enough, to achieve enough, I have
run with urgency, drowning in insecurity. But
the process of time is gradually moving me
forward so that yesterday's changes gently over-
lap into today.

---

*The Affirmation — I actively and openly
support those people I care about.*

The Reflection — While waiting at a bus stop
one day, a man and woman walked by, taking
turns guessing at what kind of guide dog I use.
"That must be a pointer," the woman said. "No,
I think it's a lab," said the man. "It's a shepherd/
lab," I said. Suddenly the woman proudly exclaimed, "See, you're wrong again!" What is it
that happens to us in our relationships that we
enjoy adding up the score of the mistakes
others make?

The Meditation — I consciously choose to notice and emphasize the ways in which others are
right. I live with others in a way that requires
and invites the best of teamwork. I may have
learned that I could temporarily inflate or validate my own self-worth by measuring and count-
ing the mistakes of others, but in the belief
system that encompasses abundance for all of
us, there is no need to dwell on the negative.

The Affirmation — It's nice to know I can outgrow what I no longer need and let it go.

The Reflection — Just as we can outgrow clothes and shoes, we can outgrow old patterns, old ways of reacting, old attractions or fears. Sometimes I'm amazed to see that I've outgrown something as a result of other changes I've made. And that process of moving forward, of developing new perceptions about what simply did not fit in my life anymore, goes on without my conscious calculation, manipulation or rehearsal.

The Meditation — I take comfort and joy in noticing what I've outgrown. There are signs of change and progress as I move through and beyond outdated aspects of my life. Old relationships, patterns, habits of reacting, even subtle thoughts can change. It's time to take risks, to let go of some things and to introduce changes that are more in keeping with my forward direction.

The Affirmation — I shuffle the deck of my own life and learn new ways to deal a better hand and play my cards.

The Reflection — Taking risks in my life is a lot like playing cards. My hand not only gets bigger, but the deck is getting larger and more cumbersome to shuffle with each new addition to my life. When something happens in my life to create a sense of "subtraction" or of loss, it feels as though I don't have enough cards to play. Then again there are those times when even some of the old and familiar cards fall out of synch, or out of the deck, and it's as if I have to play "52 Pick Up."

The Meditation — I respect the learning process I am involved in as I undergo change and risk-taking. I know that with the vulnerability of risk-taking comes exposure to my imperfections — the more ways I tackle life, the more mistakes I make. But more mistakes and more risk-taking eventually add up to more success.

The Affirmation — I get regular doses of being plugged into the juices that keep life going.

The Reflection — There is something about those special moments with selected people that gives me a feeling of being plugged into life, into myself. Such moments offer renewal, validation and new energy. I am reminded of how rich I am in my thoughts, feelings and ideas. I remember how complex I am and how there is continuity to all of the choices I make.

The Meditation — I make time to be with at least one special friend in the very near future. All it takes is the time and opportunity to truly connect with one friend who is rich in meaning for me. In such a connection, I am safe to express my own private meaning to any significant experiences I'm having. I am free to sort out my real concerns and choices. I feel plugged into the moment and life-giving energy.

The Affirmation — I take pride in a growing sense of community and my attachment to it.

The Reflection — Perhaps that old saying, "What a small world!" has more merit than is realized. I often feel a sense of importance about what commitment in relationships means. And there's a broader scale notion of what relationships mean in the context of our growing sense of community on this planet. This will require that we learn much more about what it means to be there for and with one another.

The Meditation — I appreciate my sense of community with others as I realize how we are all related in spirit. I am not alone as I face daily challenges. I continue to learn about ways to grow closer to others while still maintaining my sense of self. I realize that community is a choice, always inviting my involvement, never demanding it. I take what I like and leave the rest.

The Affirmation — I lightly happen upon those new changes that are good for me.

The Reflection — The decision I made nearly two years ago to get a working guide dog was one of those thoughts I just seemed to have happened upon. In fact, I had already constructed a well-calculated list as to why a guide dog wasn't for me. Yet when it was time to consider it again, the idea was a subtle and gentle one. So many other wonderful things have come about that way — one moment gently leading to another, then to new change that seemed to come easily.

The Meditation — I set aside the temptation to pursue my personal growth as if it were some sort of competitive event. The stress or strain also takes its toll in ways I don't need and can't afford. I ease my grip on life, my tight control on myself and others and let life gently happen.

> *The Affirmation — I offer forgiveness
> based on freedom, not based on favors.*

The Reflection — To assume that forgiveness is
a favor that we either grant to others or need
from them only feeds old patterns of unequal
power in relationships. When I feel forgiving
toward someone I feel free. I don't consider
that I'm necessarily doing someone a favor
when I forgive them. It can be hard to acccept
the forgiveness of someone else especially if
self-forgiveness is lacking.

The Meditation — I allow myself to move
beyond any temptation to forgive others out
of a self-righteous attitude. And if I am for-
given by them for something I've done, that is
their choice. Today I will begin facing the
challenge of self-forgiveness as I recognize I
am equal with others in the responsibility for
and the freedom of forgiveness.

> *The Affirmation* — *"Small world" experiences remind me of how connected and purposeful our lives really are.*

The Reflection — Suddenly I hear from someone I knew ages ago who knows someone else I haven't seen in years. Sometimes I think of how interwoven our lives become and want to get away from it all because it feels too close, too familiar. At other times I feel a tremendous sense of community. These moments bring important messages, necessary lessons and opportunities for growth.

The Meditation — Each time I suddenly find an old friend or even someone I didn't like long ago, I pay attention. I am sure to gain from reflecting on these seeming coincidences in my life. I take time to fully acknowledge, appreciate and stay tuned to the many connections and purposes, obvious and subtle, that make up my life.

> *The Affirmation — I can enjoy a new incarnation of my relationships anytime without waiting another lifetime.*

The Reflection — Sometimes I think of my relationship with my family as being in a new incarnation. There is greater mutual respect, more fun, more genuine interest in one another. Sometimes when I'm struggling to feel more forgiving toward another person or situation, I wonder, "How did I get to that place with my family?" Once I learn what mutual respect feels like, I can transfer it into more difficult present situations.

The Meditation — I am open to new incarnations. I have grown in and through relationships, learning much about myself along the way. I am not the same person I was even five years ago. I give myself room to change and grow. I accept into my life the inner wisdom, maturity and spiritual strength that come from new incarnations in my relationships.

The Affirmation — I am safe remembering the good things.

The Reflection — In order to avoid denial and the fear of some people that they might get sucked back into old self-destructive behavior, there is the temptation to harp on the negative. But fortunately there comes a time when there has been enough lamenting over the pain. I feel no shame in consciously emphasizing the good memories. It's not as though the pain gets buried or goes away. But it's time to turn the volume up on the positive in a way that is healing and enjoyable.

The Meditation — I easily let my mind flow into memory upon memory of good times with people in the past. There may be stumbling blocks over which I've tripped, but for now I just let them go and enjoy the good I remember. I allow the joy and the healing it brings to make a difference in my life.

The Affirmation — *I consciously choose to recognize life as unique, never repeating itself in the same way.*

The Reflection — It's almost morbid to suggest that life be lived and appreciated as though it were the last day or the last possible moment. Yet there is something sweet and untarnished about that sort of recognition and appreciation. Life is so fragile and so short. All there is right now is the moment.

The Meditation — I find healing and renewal as I take time to appreciate the precious gift of life. Each person who crosses my path, each child or animal can add to my sense of how fragile and sweet life is. Beyond all of my mundane concerns there is freedom as I feel myself to be a part of the big picture. I make choices that are based on my experience and find freedom in being open to life in all its precious gifts.

The Affirmation — I listen with the inner ear contained within my heart.

The Reflection — It recently dawned on me that the word ear is within the word heart. The word hear is also there. What a wonderful affirmation to remind us of the importance of listening from the heart. The language of the heart is the dialect of our emotions. But its uniqueness requires that those trying to hear us listen carefully with their inner ear.

The Meditation — I listen from my heart. It gets tempting to listen with my calculating brain. But within my heart is where my best listening takes place. My intuition, my inner child, whatever word I have for it isn't as important as my relationship with my inner self. And my growth today reflects increasing fluency in the language of my own heart and the dialect of my own feelings.

> *The Affirmation — I am open to learning with other people and open to their learning from and with me.*

The Reflection — In a recent conversation, some people said they wanted to facilitate a group with me so that we could be "co-growers." How true it is as we learn with each other in our relationships! Whether it's trying to accomplish a project at work, engage in a healthy growth process in therapy or in our intimate relationships, progress doesn't happen unless the people involved share the responsibility, energy and commitment for growth.

The Meditation — I am a student and a teacher in all of my relationships. My behavior, my silence, whatever I'm doing holds the potential of serving as lessons from which others can learn. Likewise, I learn from others. I respect what it means to be a co-grower in my relationships with individuals, families, the community, the universe and with my inner self.

The Affirmation — I let death teach me about life.

The Reflection — I became aware of people close to me dealing with Alzheimer's disease, AIDS and cancer — all in the same week. There is something about the imminence of death that helps to put much of life into perspective. Suddenly I am clearer about the importance of being more loving in the present, of being more myself, of using time and energy wisely.

The Meditation — I use my awareness of death to center me more fully into this present moment. I consider anything I can say or do that will improve the quality of my relationships. I take notice of ways to take care of things that really are my responsibilities and decide to do something about them. I will use the sense of grief and loss connected with death to encourage a clearer focus on living today.

> *The Affirmation — I am learning to be responsibly spoiled.*

The Reflection — I get so tired of people shaming themselves and others when they receive good things. "Look at how spoiled you are," they say. Does being spoiled mean being headed for trouble? We refer to spoiled food when it is rotten. Do we assume that when someone gets what they want or are lavished with more than what they had hoped for, they are sure to become rotten? The trick is to know we deserve infinite good and to enjoy it responsibly.

The Meditation — I am learning that it's okay to be spoiled, to receive many good things. I encourage others to believe this same truth for themselves. As the door opens further, I gain in wisdom about responsibly handling my abundance in direct proportion to the growing awareness of the good I'm receiving on a daily basis.

The Affirmation — I respect the obvious and hidden differences of others, knowing I also have skeletons in the closet that deserve respect.

The Reflection — Why do so many people seem to want to put others into rigid boxes, categories where they assume their behavior becomes totally predictable? This may seem to help us feel safe, but it distances everyone from us. If we take time to look in the mirror, we can't help but know that we all have warts, weaknesses, limitations.

The Meditation — I'm thankful for the moments when I realize that old assumptions can be completely reversed. These new realizations lead me to appreciate myself more fully. As I grow in accceptance of my own assumed weaknesses, I set aside rigid boxes to embrace the unique perceptions, gifts and consequences that are a part of other peoples' lives.

The Affirmation — Above all, I listen to and trust my instincts.

The Reflection — Have you heard anything like the following? "Well, these people say their reality is more accurate than my perceptions and that I'm not supposed to feel what I feel but should trust them instead." To add to it, sometimes a whole group of other people agree with the message and you're left with your own internal rumblings. How much sleep do you think anyone has ever really lost over you deciding to follow your instincts? It's really okay with the universe for you to choose.

The Meditation — My radar is my friend. I respect the signals in my body, the voices in my head, the fantasies that continue to play through my mind. In all of these behaviors, my intuition is giving me information about my experience, my needs and desires.

---

*The Affirmation — I keep my eyes open
and ready to see.*

The Reflection — There are so many statements
made which assume that the physical use of
our eyes is the only vision we have. Yet we all
say things like "I'll keep my eyes open to see
what happens" or "I see what you mean." We
see with our minds. We exercise our vision as
we allow our minds to stretch, taking in new
perceptions and creating new possibilities from
the source of our inner vision.

The Meditation — With my eyes open I am
ready to see, to consider new possibilities, to
anticipate visions never before seen. Another
way of allowing this affirmation to work for me
is to say, "I keep my mind open and ready to
experience." Today I allow my mind to stretch.
Muscles gain in strength through regular use. I
exercise the muscles of my own vision to perceive, believe and experience life in new ways.

> *The Affirmation — I take advantage of the backdoor entrances for recognizing people's positive qualities.*

The Reflection — As a child, when my friends would say how much they wanted my mother to be their mother, I always thought, "They just don't know what it's really like to live with her." Through a recent conversation with a female friend I was reminded of my mother's positive qualities. I couldn't help but think what a nice mother this friend could have been for me. Now I can see a kind, loving mother who did the best she could.

The Meditation — I use my experiences, reflections and fantasies as mirrors which tell me more about myself. What I gain or lose in one experience is information I can apply to other experiences of my life. Through the open windows of my interaction with others, I learn more about what has motivated my selection of various relationships.

> *The Affirmation — I take heart in recognizing the outdated meanings of old tapes.*

The Reflection — Once when I was struggling with an important decision, I kept thinking of all the things my mother might say about what I should do. When I finally mustered the courage to tell her, was I surprised to hear her say, "I think you should do what makes you happy." I thought, "My mother has transcended all of her own old tapes she gave me when I was growing up!"

The Meditation — When I find myself caught up in the shaming messages of old tapes, I examine whether they are relevant for me today. Just because a message was passed down doesn't mean it has to continue. I can move forward and leave such aspects of my legacy to another time and place.

> *The Affirmation — My experience is valid regardless of external circumstances or other people's intent.*

The Reflection — So often when we try to define a problem, such as sexual abuse, we weigh the behavior of others to decide whether the abuse actually took place. Unfortunately, our experience then comes to be externally judged as valid or invalid. Sexuality is so subjective. What is violation for one may not be to another. You may need to ask yourself, "Did I feel violated?" It is this subjective process of knowing your experience, your pain and your sense of shame that provides the ultimate source of validation.

The Meditation — I get beyond the need to qualify my experience by judging the actions of others. Looking at the behavior of others may help me identify my experience. I know that being awake to my experience is part of my goal. As I am willing to stand by my experience, I find freedom to move forward.

The Affirmation — I decide what creates sexual feelings for me, how I want to be sexual and with whom.

The Reflection — Have you ever heard or read about what is sexually arousing to others and thought, "What's wrong with me?" Likewise, has something aroused you and then someone else responds to your experience as though something was wrong with you? We do that to one another all the time, offering up some sort of narrow continuum of experience where only certain behaviors and experiences are considered valid or acceptable.

The Meditation — I give myself room to honestly own my sexual attractions. I give myself permission to not feel sexual towards someone or something in spite of any pressure to do otherwise. Simultaneously, I listen to my body and my emotions that give me important signals. I excuse myself from having to justify my experience by the standards and definitions of others.

The Affirmation — I actively receive and accept the comfort I deserve in light of the abuse I've survived.

The Reflection — Along with the "stiff upper lip" attitude goes an unrewarding, martyrdom-like posture requiring the sacrifice of our humanness. We are so hard on ourselves, believing that it is wrong for ourselves or anyone else to want comfort or kindness. The harder we are on others, the more revealing we are about the unrelenting way we treat ourselves.

The Meditation — I deserve all of the love, joy, comfort and kindness that is displayed toward me. I can also grow in the ability to give these to myself. I do not need to keep a stiff upper lip about my experience or act as a martyr. Yet chances are that I've been hard on myself to keep from falling into the quicksand of my old pain. Now I am learning that I have a right to be safe and to make the most of my life today.

The Affirmation — I deserve to receive good things just because I'm me and because I'm alive.

The Reflection — Are we so impoverished that we must judge ourselves and others in ways that justify the good that is received? Remember Rabbi Kushner's book, *When Bad Things Happen To Good People*? I've heard so many people reverse the title in a joking way to "When Good Things Happen To Bad People." Are we so hungry, angry or bitter that we must find ways to qualify what we receive based on need or victimhood? What if you receive more than you ever thought you even wanted? Is that okay?

The Meditation — I am learning to think and feel in ways that are more loving and less abusive towards myself as well as toward others. I know that the good that I and others receive is separate from considerations of whether it has been earned. What is truly relevant is the honest sense of self-love and self-acceptance present in my life today.

The Affirmation — *I carefully consider the emotional price of any adjustments I assume I can easily make.*

The Reflection — Recently I knew I had reached a dead end with an acquaintance at least in terms of communication. I found myself doing just enough on my part for minimal interaction. I found myself describing it as if I'd chosen to walk in spite of a limitation in one of my feet. In this relationship, one of my feet cannot fully touch the ground. By adjusting to the limitations at hand, I've chosen to walk on only part of my foot.

The Meditation — I look carefully at the adjustments I seem willing to make in order to preserve surface harmony. Am I willing to walk on only part of one or both of my feet? I am the best one for deciding what my requirements and values are and the compromises which are best for me to make versus those I'm better off putting aside.

The Affirmation — I remember to be kind to myself in all of my risk-taking.

The Reflection — I frequently marvel at just how vulnerable I feel in the midst of taking many new risks. Last week I came up with the phrase: "Sometimes I feel like my guts are on the griddle of life." You know how it feels when you're just out there, not rehearsing, not calculating, just out there. These are times when several breaks are in order.

The Meditation — I may choose to strike while the iron's hot, but I remember to take good care of myself along the way. The further I move in my own journey of personal growth, the stronger I feel about taking new and exciting risks. On the other hand, the vulnerability I've known from pain in my life is still a part of my frame of reference. This means I must find some balance between it and the strength to move forward.

> *The Affirmation — I look at the pain I've experienced that stretches beyond addictive behavior symptoms.*

The Reflection — I hear more and more people talking about sexual addiction these days. Some are making a meal out of it, pushing treatment, tossing labels around, self-diagnosing. It sounds like another disguised form of shame. Is this just one more way to control people? We've already known enough shame, dogma and external expectations. These only serve to further compound our self-inflicted recriminations for our "failure" to not live up to someone's idea of how we should get better.

The Meditation — I move beyond the tendency to label myself, to beat myself over the head about past mistakes or behavior. I stand back from the fad or fervor of recovery and look at my own experience. There is more to learn about the pain I've felt from abuse.

*The Affirmation — Even though some-
times there is only pain, I trust it as a
marker on the map that guides me towards the joy just around the corner.*

The Reflection — There have been people who
told me I was too sensitive, yet another shaming message that I was not okay. I always felt it
as a message of, "Don't feel . . . Don't be the
way you are." Being sensitive seems to mean
that sometimes the pain I experience is relent-
lessly intense. And fortunately, the potential
intensity of my joy is just as rich.

The Meditation — I realize that part of my
experience in the journey of personal growth
is pain. I know that at times I may feel or
appear too sensitive for my own good. But
being sensitive is being alive! I remind myself
that there will be times once again of total joy.
And there will be many more times when a
mixture of pain and joy will be the norm.

The Affirmation — I am learning what I need to do and experience for living in an atmosphere of safe trust.

The Reflection — It's hard to learn when we feel our trust is being violated or when we've violated someone else's. Having been violated in any way doesn't automatically mean knowing how not to violate the trust of others. Trust can be violated in ways so subtle that they are hard to fully recognize and appreciate. Strengthening our own sense of integrity — which is directly tied to resolving our shame — is the best place to start.

The Meditation — I am coming to learn more of what my experience is when my trust is violated and growing to understand what I need to do or not do to maintain an atmosphere of trust for others. The most important relationship I maintain is the growing one with myself, especially when it comes to shaping and defining the values and beliefs that determine my personal boundaries.

The Affirmation — I embrace the courage it takes to honor and stand by my values.

The Reflection — In a sense, our values serve to reflect the outline of our past experience. They also help shape our future choices. Staying in touch with our values is hard enough. And remaining honest about our values can mean standing alone in the face of a crowd. This requires our being able to appreciate our individual uniquenesses. It is also inversely related to the extent to which we have healed from our shame.

The Meditation — I respect my values. Compromise is a valuable aspect of healthy relationships, but not so when I allow compromising that chips away at or violates my own values. I no longer have to be a victim to the rules and whims of other people. Today I embrace the courage to be who I am and to honor the values that free me from shame.

*The Affirmation — I take care of myself
in spite of everything.*

The Reflection — I was making homemade
vegetable juice the other morning and began
reflecting on how valuable and important it is
for me to do this kind of healthy activity. It
reminds me that I am still standing by myself,
with myself in the midst of change. Drinking
that fresh juice gives me a concrete sense of
being connected to the spirit and the earth.
This is also an important ritual in nurturance.

The Meditation — I recognize ways in which I
can take care of myself and am willing to
pledge my allegiance to do so. I go that extra
mile for myself in doing things that are positive,
healthy and self-nurturant. I take time to notice
my heightened spirits and energy level as I reap
the benefits of taking care of myself.

The Affirmation — I am part of a large chain of giving and receiving.

The Reflection — Often I hear statements like "But I don't know what I can give you in return" or, "I've given a lot to them and they haven't given me anything that matches my efforts." It's important to remember that relationships are not based on a 50-50 split. Things are not going to come back to us anytime soon, nor even from the same person to whom we have given. There are no straight lines when it comes to giving and receiving in relationships.

The Meditation — When I give and someone else receives, they will have opportunities to give. Although a sense of reciprocity is somewhat important, I may not have chances to give to the same people who have given to me. Today I remain open to the flow of giving and receiving.

The Affirmation — I center myself and trust the positive effects that follow.

The Reflection — Meditation time may or may not be eventful. It may be a time of insight and rich experience or very low key and quiet-feeling. What counts is what you have in the bank to draw upon later as inner sight. Ideas, calm, wisdom — these are all available and are much more likely to come when you are truly able to be receptive.

The Meditation — I anticipate the positive effects of the time I take for myself in meditation. New creative ideas, a more lasting and refreshing threshold for dealing with people, an inner calm that truly is genuine — I expect and acknowledge these to be a part of my experience. Whatever I did for myself yesterday will help me today. What I do for myself today can only work in my best interests tomorrow.

> *The Affirmation — I use language that is in line with my integrity, my values and my deserved self-esteem.*

The Reflection — Have you ever thought about how many of our common expressions are derogatory phrases about our own bodies, the bodies of the opposite sex or bodily functions? Perhaps at an unconscious level the continual use of such phrases reflects uncomfortable feelings about physical intimacy or our own body-image. For those of us who have been sexually violated or exploited, hearing such phrases woven nonchalantly into everyday conversation can only heighten our levels of shame.

The Meditation — I notice my own and others' language about bodies. Today I strive to use words in ways that support positive feelings about bodies — my own and those of others. I am growing in my ability to respect and honor my sexuality. This includes an appreciation of all my bodily functions.

The Affirmation — I give myself permission to know and set my own pace for disclosing what happened to me.

The Reflection — For many of us who grew up in an abusive environment, there is a sense that "something happened." In a time where self-help groups are springing up for every kind of problem imaginable, we may feel a certain pressure to "tell one, tell all." We might experience feelings not unlike early childhood violation in response to this. We build defenses for a reason. And we treat ourselves lovingly when we respect our own timing about such private disclosures.

The Meditation — I give myself room to disclose my story in a way that is loving towards myself and respectful of my defenses, knowing I must be able to trust others with the depth of my emotion. I honor the bricks in the wall, removing them at my own pace in my own way, ever mindful of gradual, safe change.

The Affirmation — I check my emotional balance, noticing the trust in friends I have accumulated in my personal bank of emotional health.

The Reflection — My friendship with Michael (friend and editor of this book) is one that tells me how much trust I have accumulated in my emotional health bank account. Over three years, I notice how easily I can laugh at my mistakes, feel safe to consider new ideas, disagree without feeling threatened or defensive. When I look at some of my newer relationships, I wonder why I feel so vulnerable and nervous.

The Meditation — I do not have to rush into new relationships. Looking at some of my healthier friendships, I can see places where my trust has developed over time, where I have felt centered and safe enough to be myself. Today I embrace healthy friendships that support the foundations for my growth and integrity.

> *The Affirmation — I trust I'll not miss things that are right and important and that I'll get what I need.*

The Reflection — It's so easy to get caught up in the feeling of being behind the times. Sometimes we say to ourselves, "Look at all the years, the experiences, opportunities that have gone by me." So much of our childhoods were spent hearing how we didn't measure up. So it's not hard to understand why we go around thinking, "I've done it all wrong. Now I need to hurry and catch up so I don't miss anything."

The Meditation — I'm open to new experiences. I do not need to sabotage my progress by being fixed on what I might have missed. I do get what I need. Right now I can name a number of things that are in place within my life as resources. I trust I will be directed to what I need that's important at the time it's needed.

The Affirmation — I speak about the things I am most in need of learning.

The Reflection — The words we use when writing or speaking are metaphors and symbols of what's important in our lives. Inherent in our grammatical structure is our belief system, our philosophical outlooks, our fears and projections. As I write this book, I notice how often I choose to write about issues that are relevant for me at the time. I have also listened to the wisdom I receive when writing and pass it along in these words so that I too can learn from what I say.

The Meditation — Today I begin to listen to the themes that continue to come up in my conversations and in my thoughts. What is it I can do or learn about the issues that continue to affect me? I use my own language to reflect on my experience as landmarks, mirrors and doorways to the important lessons in life.

The Affirmation — I do not compartmentalize my experience before I have gained from the fullness of it.

The Reflection — People categorize their experience, particularly when it pertains to affection and sexual expression. It seems that if one feels sexual, then sexual behavior is expected. If one doesn't feel sexual, then affection is expressed in clear, rigid lines. Have you ever noticed how people hug when they want to make sure sexual behavior is not part of the relationship? It's courtesy hugging with lots of distance.

The Meditation — I trust the fluid process of my experience. I allow myself to feel sexual and affectionate, without the need to sell myself short with rigid, restrictive boundaries. I can safely remain open to a broad continuum of experience and desires. All experiences lead to better self-understanding and decisions about relationships.

> *The Affirmation — Love and goodness
> wait for me around the corner . . . far
> beyond what I can imagine right now.*

The Reflection — It's so easy to project into the
future and let our fears dictate the course of
events. We convince ourselves that we're feeling
sure about what will and will not take place,
that we're being realistic. Yet how often have
we been surprised to find that opportunities
came when we least expected, and we were
glad to be in their path? We tend to call those
things luck.

The Meditation — The surprises I receive are
ways in which I can take note of my projected
self-worth. Instead of being tempted to run
myself down all the time, I can use the good I
receive as a means for building myself up. I can
expect positive surprises, joyous opportunities
and possibilities that haven't yet been imagined
in the vision of my own mind.

The Affirmation — *My own perceptions and experiences are valid and important for me first and foremost.*

The Reflection — I showed this book before it was published to a couple of people to get their feedback. The assumptions these folks had about the book are interesting. Some assumed it addresses sexual abuse and others said they didn't see much of that in it. The meaning I find in it is how I use what I find outside of myself and combine it with my own experience.

The Meditation — I need not wait for the definitions or perceptions of others before knowing that my own are valid. My perceptions are important. They are my tickets to future decisions and experiences. As I stand in the doorway of new learning, discovery and healing, my perceptions provide the map for stepping over the threshold and going in the right direction.

The Affirmation — I don't just talk about growth, I am growing each day and remain committed to the journey.

The Reflection — Sometimes giving lip service to a new behavior is an important first step in trying it on. Talking about a desired change as if it's already a part of you is a way to test the waters. It can often be one way of creating and accepting the possibility of new behaviors. But beyond talking is the need to take action, to put a concrete plan for implementing a new behavior or attitude in your life on a daily basis.

The Meditation — Today I notice the ways in which I am growing beyond the mere words and jargon of personal growth guruism. My growth is revealed in the example I set with my behavior, to the extent I put my insights and beliefs into action. I commit myself to active growth beyond lip service and set the stage for new capabilities.

> *The Affirmation — I stretch without
> straining to reach for more of life and
> the positive energy it holds.*

The Reflection — Stretching is something we
often do to start the new day, to take a needed
break. It is part of revitalizing, relaxing, letting
go of tension. Straining, on the other hand, is
pushing past the limits in a way that inflicts
painful pressure. Doesn't it make sense that if
we exceed our emotional flexibility, we run the
risk of damaging our emotional muscle?

The Meditation — I stretch to greet the new
day, the new tasks at hand, knowing I am reaching further for the good I deserve. As I stretch
my muscles and my mind, I feel a surge of
willingness to let go of tensions, anxieties or
any pockets of garbage I may have been carrying around. I stretch, knowing it's time I allow
myself to fully extend my abilities and desires
out into the universe.

> *The Affirmation — I turn up the volume of ways to know I am loved from deep within myself.*

The Reflection — Feeling loved from deep within is a marvelous catalyst for bringing out those qualities we are often striving so hard to achieve. We talk about trying to be forgiving, to be playful and kind. But we simply don't express these things easily. But have you ever noticed how easily those qualities are expressed as part of you when you are consciously aware of feeling deeply loved?

The Meditation — Today I freely enjoy the love others express towards me. Compliments, nurturance, gifts, kind gestures — I accept them for what they are and let the positive energy and regard expressed by others work for me. As I laugh more freely and fully, play more spontaneously, I feel even more freedom to loosen my grip on the balance between giving and receiving.

The Affirmation — I trust myself to make clear choices about relationships.

The Reflection — Sometimes I feel that problems in a relationship stem from my own inner turmoil. I proceed as though the key is always to magically become open and receptive to everyone who crosses my path. Suddenly it dawns on me, after I have extended an attitude of friendliness, that my original perception was right. Here is a person I really don't want in my personal life, no matter how loving and accepting I may feel.

The Meditation — I work towards allowing myself to discern and discriminate my honest feelings and choices about relationships. As I have moved away from the shame-based messages of childhood, I have grown stronger in my capability for making decisions from a basis of strength, and can own the freedom and responsibility of my choices.

> *The Affirmation — I enjoy the fullness of my attitude towards an appetite for life.*

The Reflection — Warned not to be greedy, egotistical or grandiose, how often have we been secretly filled with guilt and shame about what we hoped we finally deserve to receive? Yet I maintain that it isn't the amount we want or the intense desire to receive it that is the problem. It's the fear that eats at our fragile threads of self-worth, telling us we're not good enough to enjoy what we have.

The Meditation — I have a big appetite for life. I want a lot and am growing to feel okay about the amount of life I am learning to receive. My desires for more tell me that I am getting ready to embrace the abundance I deserve. Today I give up any lingering feelings that life is meager and become receptive to prosperity and fulfillment.

The Affirmation — I'm okay alone.

The Reflection — Recently it dawned on me that not choosing to become involved with any of the people who are attracted to me would mean I stay where I am — with myself. I may not be as able to build the life I would really like to have with someone else either. It's not easy to listen to these two seemingly discrepant voices and also reconcile the signals of others. Better to focus on my own choices and responses and be with myself.

The Meditation — It's nice to have someone around, but I find my own company to be enjoyable and quite nurturing to my spirit. As I let unwanted opportunities go by, I rest assured that I do not need to run after anyone just because they're there, reaching out to me. I only need to make a commitment when I consider the outcome to be good and right for me.

The Affirmation — I'm a little/big, big/ little person.

The Reflection — Perhaps one of the most powerful and heart-warming aspects of the adult children's movement is its full recognition of the paradox we live with on a daily basis. We have adult, "big people" bodies inside of which live "little people" feelings, fears, shame and confusion. We develop intimate relationships, yet feel like awkward 14-year-olds on their first date.

The Meditation — I am a little person inside this adult body. I am as equally capable of childlike playfulness, love and joy as I am of hurt and childish feelings. Sometimes there are "big lessons" to learn, big decisions to make and strength to find even when I don't feel strong. Today I appreciate a balance of my bigness and smallness as I experience the fullness of who I am and what my life is about.

The Affirmation — I pay attention to the signals I receive of anything in my life that's not working. The signals are there for a reason.

The Reflection — The modem for my computer started making some strange noises last night that clearly sounded like trouble. I thought of continuing to push it to see if I could get it to work. Finally I decided that my intuition is with me for a reason and the noise was a message to me that it was malfunctioning. The modem is just an inanimate object, albeit an important link for me.

The Meditation — I listen to signals I receive of problems with my things, my relationships or my health. Symptoms and signals are not merely there to annoy me, they are there to get my attention. At the outset they need me to notice what's wrong and at a deeper level there may be other things for me to notice.

346

> *The Affirmation — I take advantage of the oppportunities I find in my willingness to shift gears.*

The Reflection — Sometimes I don't want to shift gears because I have a set idea of how things are supposed to be. And when they're not, I feel as though I'm going backwards or something is being kept from me. Getting past old scripts is not easy. But when I do, it's as if the possibilities multiply in direct proportion to my willingness to shift gears. It's not a matter of other people keeping things from me; it's a case of my keeping things from myself.

The Meditation — What will be the moments today for me to shift gears? I will remember to notice that they may in fact be opportunities, not merely disadvantages. I notice such moments as signals that I can stretch and experience my life in expanded ways.

> *The Affirmation — I let sexual energy work for me in creative ways.*

The Reflection — Sometimes I talk with people who wish they didn't feel sexual. They want to turn their desire off because they believe it's dirty or a great inconvenience. I believe our sexuality and its energy are there for a reason. One does not have to indulge just for the sake of satisfying urges, but sexual energy is a major part of our life-force. It can work as a catalyst for growing both internally and externally.

The Meditation — I let my sexual energy move me in ways that allow me to let others know more about who I am as a person, fully alive with feelings and issues yet to be explored. I let my energy spur me on to test my muscles, both in my ability to grow in my beliefs as well as in my level of activity.

> *The Affirmation — I endorse and embrace the passionate and romantic aspects of life and love.*

The Reflection — I am concerned about how sterile we become when we want to make sure we're not being co-dependent or neurotic. Certainly we want to make sure we're moving beyond old scripts and outdated stereotypes that limit us and our relationships. But the problem comes when we don't allow for spontaneity because we're so busy measuring and calculating ourselves and others.

The Meditation — I do have desires, romantic dreams, fantasies. I let these emerge in my consciousness and let their vibrance work for me. The challenge is to live with all the awareness I'm gaining in ways that help me to be more responsible with my choices and decisions. I strive to become open and alive while discriminating and wise.

The Affirmation — I decide to face forward instead of constantly looking over my shoulder.

The Reflection — So often I find that as soon as I loosen my grip on whatever I assume to be the controls of life, the goodies come to me in amazing ways. When I am least expecting or trying to anticipate, there it is, another one of life's surprises! It's as though I merely needed to get out of the way so there would be room for their entrance. For a lot of us, the low self-worth and shame we have struggled with has only kept us looking back over our shoulders, making sure life wouldn't surprise us.

The Meditation — I look at how I can appreciate today and focus on the tasks at hand. Today, tomorrow, any time now, surprises will knock at my door. And the best part is, I'll be able to take advantage of their momentum and energy like a child thrilled with the delight of newness.

> *The Affirmation — I find treasures in moments where old friendships become renewed and take on new meaning.*

The Reflection— With the addition of modem (computer) communication in my life, I find greater joy in staying in touch with someone who was an old friend. Our past friendship was not one where I often considered the importance of reaching out in heartfelt ways. Now, reuniting in a new way, I disclose, enjoy and reach out, treasuring this opportunity to have a new friendship.

The Meditation — I look at my relationships and notice any that are part of my life in new ways. Are there ways I want them to be different from what they were in the past? I look wisely and appreciatively at those new/old friendships that are here in my life and choose ways to enjoy and learn both from and with them.

The Affirmation — I let myself vulnerably and completely reach for love in opportune moments.

The Reflection — I always enjoy the way my dog Lyndi reaches for my love. She's under the desk as I write, stretching her neck up for me to pet her as I sit down. She plops herself near me when she wants my attention, and isn't afraid to show me both audibly and nonverbally what she wants and how she wants it.

The Meditation — I am ready to receive the love I want and deserve. I allow myself to ask, show, teach chosen friends or loved ones what is pleasurable for me in accepting love and expressing my vulnerability. I express with my body. I express with my silence, rather than in an assertive verbal mode. In short, I am more me, more alive and less calculating, less sterile. My choices may not always be correct, but I am whole and much freer wherever I go.

The Affirmation — I focus my attention on what I want to accomplish and it does get done.

The Reflection — Sometimes I'm involved in so many things at once I wonder how I will get any one thing finished. I find that all I need to do is decide it is time to get one of these things done, make it a priority, and what do you know? It gets finished! This doesn't necessarily mean it gets finished today. Some things take sustained, prioritized effort. There's an old saying that, "A man with a point in every direction is the same as a man with no point at all."

The Meditation — I ask myself what my true priorities are. As I focus my attention on one goal at a time, I get going on things and I can embrace a momentum that supports getting to the finish line. I can take control of my time and my goals. My life today is manageable.

> *The Affirmation — I recognize the dif-
> ference between the message and the
> way in which it's communicated.*

The Reflection — I react to messages that are
communicated without adequate respect for
self-esteem or personal boundaries. This does
not mean that there's no room for the message
itself, but that there is a better way to communicate it. Too often I hear therapists debating
over the role of confrontation in therapy or
individuals debating on outspokenness in relationships. There is a way to say anything. And
it makes all the difference in the world.

The Meditation — I consider the way I say
things, the ways in which things are said to me
and how I have felt about them in the past.
Messages are received by me every day, some
more directly than others. I consider better
ways to communicate more lovingly.

The Affirmation — *I continue to both ask myself and answer the question of what's important.*

The Reflection — We all have days from time to time that seem to be ruled by Murphy's Law. They are not a lot of fun, but they can provide an interesting opportunity to ask and answer the question of what's important. There may be a variety of signs that what we feel is important is not what's happening. Here I am presented with an opportunity to assess whether my goals are what I have been declaring them to be or if they have changed.

The Meditation — I listen to the messages in my environment and ask myself what really is important. It may be that what's important to me is not being reinforced by others, by the events of my daily life. This may call for re-assessment of my goals or of the places where I am looking to find support for them.

The Affirmation — I take time to lie back and let others do the work.

The Reflection — There is a lot to be said for letting others do their best work and give their best to life. It is so tempting and yet so draining to assume we must always be in there — giving, performing. Yet, to passively receive is an important part of giving and is vital to our emotional health. If we never let others give to us, we rob them of the chance to love us and we cheat ourselves out of nurturance.

The Meditation — I allow myself to get out of the driver's seat and give others a chance to give to me and to life. It is good for me to accept nurturance and to experience a sense of synergy as we each take our turn at giving and receiving. By blending the best of ourselves together, we can move beyond what can be accomplished as separate individuals.

The Affirmation — I allow things to be "sometimes" true for me.

The Reflection — It is so tempting to look for permanent answers, for insights that can be forever true in every situation. But what is true for me this moment may change at any time or it may be true most of the time but may still carry exceptions. One of the biggest barriers to our own growth and recovery is thinking we have discovered THE truth or THE answer.

The Meditation — I need not be threatened by shifts in my perceptions or in my experience. Instead, I take these shifts as invitations to stretch or broaden my awareness. In moments where I allow this expansion, I gain wisdom that adds flexibility to my life and to what I am able to contribute to the lives of others.

> *The Affirmation — I am completely hon-*
> *est with myself and discretely honest with*
> *others.*

The Reflection — Often I hear people talking
about honesty as though it's written in stone
somewhere that we should always be honest
with others. I maintain that it is only required
for me to be honest with myself. I am the one
who needs to know what I'm feeling and thinking, what I'm wanting or needing. There may
be a place for honesty in my relationships, but
it is always second to how honest I am with
myself first.

The Meditation — I listen to what my feelings
and thoughts are, being careful not to censure
them by anticipating what anyone else will
think. I learn about being honest with others in
ways that continue to teach me to respect my
own personal integrity, boundaries and emotional needs. Honesty to myself is most important to my emotional well-being.

The Affirmation — I trust the universe to keep me growing on the cutting edge of life.

The Reflection — Sometimes things don't go the way I want them to. I try to use these times to reflect on how the universe is teaching me once again that I'm not meant to obsess but to flow with the pace of life. At the cutting edge, I am alone when filled with doubt, but more at home when I trust in the big picture.

The Meditation — Sometimes I feel I'm going along with life by the seat of my pants. I can't predict or plan and am left to wait and trust. I can use these opportunities to strengthen my spiritual muscles, to build my faith in a larger picture that is not weighed down by old, repetitive doubts and worn-out, cynical beliefs. I can remember to trust that I'm part of a larger plan.

> *The Affirmation — I use this holiday season as an opportunity to celebrate the birth of my own inner child and honor the new life I have created in recovery.*

The Reflection — One doesn't have to be Christian to enjoy Christmas. It can be a time to celebrate the birth of your own inner child. It can be used as a way of bringing out one's childlike spirit to enjoy the glitter and excitement. It can be a time to play, to sing, to take risks in reaching out to people, to work on your own ability to receive more comfortably.

The Meditation — I consider during this time of the year what it means to live with a childlike spirit — an attitude of hope, of promise, of gratitude for the discovery of my own inner child. Today my child within lives surrounded by the loving nurture that was not a part of my original childhood. My inner child has come alive and joins me at this time of year to celebrate.

The Affirmation — There is so much more to me than the shame I feel.

The Reflection — We carry our shame as though it is a big secret, as though no one else experiences it. We have an ugly feeling about ourselves, repetitive thoughts of unworthiness and insecurity. At a deeper level, we humans have these experiences in common. But our collective sense of shame is only one factor in many that has shaped who we are. We are far more than that.

The Meditation — No matter how old or big it has become, I am more than my shame. I am freer today than I was before I began to reach out for personal growth. Somehow, I knew I was worthy of something better. Now I am working to change all of those patterns that have encouraged me to harbor thoughts and feelings of insecurity.

> *The Affirmation — I decide when it is*
> *appropriate for me to be* for, *rather than*
> against, *giving.*

The Reflection — Forgiveness is one of those
places where we often get stuck. We either
think we "must" forgive everyone for everything
or not forgive because it might merely be a form
of denial. I heard a nun once say that it's up to
us to forgive ourselves and up to God to forgive
everyone else. Anger or grief must be resolved
in order to forgive ourselves or others. Otherwise we can end up staying stuck in resentment
and let our lives be ruled by negativity.

The Meditation — Today I am growing freer to
decide when it is appropriate for me to forgive.
Choosing to be *for* giving, rather than *against*
it keeps me open to recognizing what's best
for me. When I am *for* giving, it reflects openness and receptivity to life. I then know there
will always be good and generosity in the
universe for me.

> *The Affirmation* — *I work to improve myself in every relationship, knowing that my patterns are with me wherever and with whomever I go.*

The Reflection — How often you hope that some special person in your life will be spared some attributes of your character — moodiness, angry outbursts, petty need for control, etc. Perhaps you believe you have been able to successfully put all of your ugliness in the past. So now you think this person will only get the best of your attitude. Wouldn't it be nice if it were that easy?

The Meditation — As I become so much more myself, I appreciate the fluid process of my ways. I cannot separate myself into little pockets where everything is calculated and rehearsed. I am willing to improve myself and my relationships as I act with integrity and communicate with respect and honesty.

The Affirmation — I am honest with myself about my projections, remembering that often there is more going on than I might assume.

The Reflection — There is a certain amount of freedom in knowing that there is a difference between projection and the truth. There are more doors, more possibilities and better opportunities that can spring forth just by merely remembering that what I'm tempted to assume may not be all that's going on, may not even be true.

The Meditation — While I may choose to think in noncluttered ways, keeping my life simple, I can also keep my mind open. There is safety in gathering a bunch of assumptions together and putting a lid on them. But there is often a loss of valuable learning and opportunity. I stay open and receptive, knowing that there is more to any situation than I am tempted to project and assume.

> *The Affirmation — I trust the universe to support my true selfhood and in turn I do the same for others.*

The Reflection — It can be so scary to give people the room they seek. "What if they abandon me?" Isn't that the bottom-line fear? But to hold someone captive is just one more expression of how old patterns of abuse are lived out. At the core of these feelings is a lack of belief in one's ability to be loved and wanted, so we tend to believe that the answer lies in controlling and maintaining power over others.

The Meditation — I trust the universe to give me and those I care about what we need. If someone isn't what I want them to be in my life, perhaps there are other lessons for me to learn. Perhaps they are showing me that I can expand my understanding of them, of myself, of life. Perhaps it's time for me to open up to the possibility that there is something or someone better for me.

The Affirmation — I am safe to consider my life as part of a bigger picture that reflects through the universe.

The Reflection — I notice that I have more consistent patience with my dog Lyndi than I have had with anyone or anything in the past. I still praise her with genuine zeal when she does something as menial as relieving herself. Yet I can remember when I was too caught up with one or other detail, lost in obsessive concern in any given moment, where my inconsistent presence could leave anyone in a relationship with me wondering who the hell I was.

The Meditation — I am growing in so many wonderful ways. I can see more fully now that my life is part of a big picture. I have more patience, energy and a sense of being alive that I can use to focus my attention on the present. I am resilient, vitally alive and involved with life in a way that is helpful to others and joyous to myself.

About The Author

Deborah Melaney Hazelton is a licensed mental health counselor who created InnerSight Unlimited and currently serves as President and Founder. InnerSight Unlimited is a consulting, counseling and educational organization offering services to the general public and the professional community.

Debbie has been involved extensively in her own personal growth and has worked professionally for 17 years in the areas of self-improvement, human potential and development, recovery and human sexuality, including sexual abuse issues. She holds Bachelor's and Master's degrees in psychology and has completed advanced graduate training (Education Specialist Degree) in guidance and counseling (from West Georgia College, Carrollton, Georgia).

Most recently, Debbie served as the Contributing Editor for U.S. Journal periodicals (including *Changes* magazine, *FOCUS* magazine and *The U.S. Journal of Drug & Alcohol Dependence*). The former Outreach Coordinator for Health Communications, Inc. and U.S. Journal, Inc., she was also the editor of *CONTACT* Newsletter, an information service of these two organizations. Debbie's professional career has included positions as college-level instructor, coordinator of student services for people living with disabilities and consultant to the program in human sexuality at the University of Miami Medical School, Department of Family Medicine. She can also be heard in the local and nationally-syndicated radio feature series which she created, entitled, "InnerSight Unlimited," that focuses on attitudes about disability and differentness.

If you would like additional information about InnerSight Unlimited and Debbie Hazelton's availability as a speaker, consultant or trainer for your community group or professional organization, please call or write directly to:

InnerSight Unlimited
265 South Federal Highway, Suite 125
Deerfield Beach, FL 33441
PHONE: (305) 480-6014